W9-CDY-958

ASCENSION

THE 99 HANDBOOK

A Catholic Guide to a Life of Faith

Mark Hart with Joel Stepanek

ASCENSION

West Chester, Pennsylvania

Ascension
Post Office Box 1990
West Chester, PA 19380
1-800-376-0520
ascensionpress.com

Printed in the United States of America
19 20 21 22 23 5 4 3 2 1

ISBN 978-1-950784-01-1

Contents

Foreword

A couple of years ago, I came across a shocking and disturbing statistic. Forty-seven percent of American Catholics were not certain that one can have a personal relationship with God.

Think about that.

Almost half of all baptized Catholics in the United States wonder whether or not they can have a relationship with God. This means there are millions of people who have been baptized— that is, they have become God's adopted sons and daughters— who believe that this relationship *isn't even possible*.

Why is this? What can account for this total misunderstanding of the Christian faith? How could we have arrived here?

There might be any number of answers: lackluster religious education classes, whether in CCD or even in Catholic schools; the relatively low percentage of Catholic families who attend Mass every Sunday; uninspiring and uninformative preaching; the decrease in the number of priests and religious sisters; and our increasingly secular culture.

I wonder, though, if the source is even deeper. I wonder if the source of this uncertainty about the possibility of a relationship with God comes from the depths of our hearts.

Through the wonders of modern technology, we are more connected than ever before. The Internet, text messaging, video calls, and social media have given us the ability to be in a constant state of interaction. Yet recent studies reveal that we have actually become more isolated than ever. We are online, but does anyone actually see us? We have a social media profile, but does anyone truly know us? We have a lot of "friends" or "followers," but is there anyone out there who really cares about us?

In the midst of life's struggles and sufferings, we may even ask these questions about God. Does God see me? Does he know me? Does he even care about me? The Christian faith, of course, provides our minds with the assurance that God is omniscient and all-loving, so we are given the assurance that God does indeed see us, know us, and love us, but do we really *believe* this? Does the reality of God's love for each of us penetrate to the deepest depths of our heart? Do we really accept that we are called to a personal relationship with the One who created us?

In my ministry as a priest, I have come to see that one troubling issue comes up again and again: a majority of Catholics—including many who attend Mass regularly—do not believe that God loves them. Now, they have heard that God loves them. They have read in the Bible that God loves them. They may have even be tempted to believe that God loves them. But most do not really *believe* that God loves them.

Why is this? The reasons vary with the individual. Some struggle with certain sins, and they do not see how God could love them with all of their imperfections. Others know that they do not pray as much as they should or feel that they don't measure up to those who are more generous and patient than they are. Maybe they see themselves as worthy of being tolerated by God rather than loved.

So many—even practicing Christians—reach this sad conclusion: *God wouldn't want to be in relationship with someone like me.*

And yet …

… Jesus shares a number of stories in the Gospels that strike at the heart of this lie that festers in our hearts, showing us how much God truly loves us and wants to be in relationship with each of us.

In Luke, chapter fifteen, he tells his disciples about the joy a woman had over finding a lost coin. This woman is so happy at locating her misplaced coin that she invites her friends to celebrate with her. And Jesus says, "Just so, I tell you, there will be more joy in heaven over one sinner who repents than over ninety-nine righteous persons who have no need of repentance" (Luke 15:10).

Later in the same chapter of Luke's Gospel, Jesus shares the famous parable of the Prodigal Son—the story of a stubborn and selfish young man who demands his inheritance from his father, then abandons his family and wastes what he has received on loose living. Finally, when he had spent everything and was starving, he comes to his senses and decides to return home, seeking his father's forgiveness. His father is ecstatic at his change of heart and embraces him. To his older son, who is angry that his father is so easily forgiving his brother, he says, "It was fitting to make merry and be glad, for this your brother was dead, and is alive; he was lost, and is found" (Luke 15:32).

Then, Jesus reveals his own heart when he talks about the sheep who leaves the flock. Out of one hundred sheep, one walks away from the other ninety-nine and becomes lost. Because the good shepherd knows his sheep and cares for them, he leaves the rest of the flock and pursues the one that is lost. His love for each of his sheep spurs him on. He pursues the lost sheep relentlessly, to bring it back into the fold (see Matthew 18:12–14; Luke 15:3–7).

As Jesus explains, "And when he [the good shepherd] has found it, he lays it on his shoulders, rejoicing. And when he comes home, he calls together his friends and his neighbors, saying to them, 'Rejoice with me, for I have found my sheep which was lost.' Just so, I tell you, there will be more joy in heaven over one sinner who repents than over ninety-nine righteous persons who need no repentance" (Luke 15:5–7).

The ninety-nine—the one.

We are God's flock. He *sees* each of us. He *knows* each of us. He *loves* each of us. He *seeks* a relationship with each of us. We *all* matter to him.

By reading this book, my hope is you will come to know—and accept—this profound truth. Whether you are one of the ninety-nine who has never wandered off or the one who has wandered far from home, you are loved by God and called to a relationship with him.

Believe it!

Fr. Mike Schmitz

The 99 Manifesto

There is something amazing happening in the Catholic Church right now.

Around the world, people just like you and me are talking to others about the transformation they have experienced in their lives from their relationship with Jesus.

In other words, they are *evangelizing*. They are spreading the Good News of Christ to others.

It is happening! Somewhere out there, at this very moment, someone is sharing the Gospel—and the Holy Spirit is moving in and through the hearts of those hearing it.

Perhaps you readily and often share Jesus and his saving message with others.

Maybe you are totally at ease telling others about how God is active in your life.

Or, like many, maybe you are afraid of others' reaction or feel it is not your place to be preachy, or fear coming across the wrong way. Maybe you want to share but lack the words.

Perhaps you are afraid that no one really cares about your story.

In the end, though, the question is not whether God is working in your life. He is. The question is whether you can recognize his role in your story and are willing to share it with others. This is your invitation to share your story.

Evangelization wasn't something most Catholics talked about until recently. Then, when more of us finally did start talking about it, we quickly realized it was something we were not really sure about. We knew the information, but we weren't exactly sure how to share it.

With so many people today being interested in spirituality and finding meaning in life, why is it so difficult for many of us to talk about God and Jesus, even with those who are close to us?

This question led to years of praying, thinking, and planning— and ultimately to the development of *The 99,* a new system of evangelization for Catholics.

The 99 is made up of three parts, that are designed to help you quickly and easily organize an effective, ongoing evangelization effort in your parish and community.

The centerpiece of the program is *The 99 Experience,* a short series of inspirational video presentations that will spark conversation, inspire prayer, and awaken the call of God's love within you. Bring people together to watch and discuss these videos and build new relationships with them.

The simplest way to offer *The 99 Experience* is through a mission series. For example, through a three-part parish evangelization mission. In most cases, organizing *The 99 Experience* events requires a dedicated team, so we have developed *The 99 Masterclass.*

The 99 Masterclass draws on the expertise of a group of experienced evangelists to help form your team and aid you in preparing to host *The 99 Experience.* This series of short, engaging videos paired with your guide will provide your team with tested and proven principles of evangelization to give your team a framework to build from, rather than having to start from scratch.

The third part of *The 99* is the book you are holding your hands, *The 99 Handbook.*

This short book makes the case that a life of faith is necessary, reasonable, and rewarding. It also explains how evangelization is a critical part of a life of faith. *The 99 Handbook* works as an ideal follow up to *The 99 Experience.*

By offering all participants in *The 99 Experience* a copy of *The 99 Handbook* and inviting them to join a book study in the weeks following, you give them the opportunity to develop the relationships they began during *The 99 Experience.* From these relationships, new communities can grow in your parish–and an increasing number of people can become engaged in the work of evangelization.

Those who participate in *The 99 Experience* and book study may then go through *The 99 Masterclass* and become part of your evangelization team, ultimately helping to offer *The 99 Experience* to even more people in your parish or community.

As you experience the different aspects of *The 99* you may be not only inspired and energized, but also you might be challenged in your mission. Most of all, our prayer is that you feel called: called to a life of faith with Jesus and his Church and inspired with an urgency to share that life with others.

Thank you for joining us in *The 99* movement, introducing even more people to Jesus, so he can touch their hearts and transform their lives.

Do not be content being "part of the 99." Be the "one" God works through. Be the "one" and go out and find the next "one."

Intro

I have a habit of repeatedly touching my wedding ring—every day, many times a day.

I rarely even notice I'm doing it. Sometimes, though, I will notice it, say in the middle of a conversation or as I am waiting to check out at the grocery store.

I have only misplaced my wedding ring a couple of times, but I've rarely felt an anxiety like I've felt in those moments. As soon as I became aware that my wedding ring wasn't on my finger, I dropped everything and commenced a full search. I retraced my steps. I asked people if they had seen it (of course, not my wife!). I searched pockets, car seats, and desks. I have even dismantled the plumbing in my sink to look if it was stuck in a drain trap.

You might think you have an idea of what my wedding ring looks like. Perhaps you are picturing a diamond encrusted, solid gold piece that glimmers like the sun in the right light. You may think this ring is so valuable that I repeatedly touch it to ensure that it is always there.

Actually, it is a black tungsten ring that cost less than $250. While there are thousands of rings like mine, the one on my finger truly is unique. This is the ring I wore on my wedding day—so it is special and unrepeatable. If I ever lose it, no replacement ring would have the history attached to it.

Now that is worth stopping everything to search for.

What in your life is worth stopping everything to search for? What could you lose that would be so valuable everything would go into lockdown mode until it was found? What responsibilities would you put off to find it? What would you trade to get it back?

The anxiety over something lost is fundamental to human experience. We do not get worried about losing something we can easily replace. While we may be upset about the cost of replacing it, this is about as far as our anxiety goes.

Some things are worth more. Some things are irreplaceable.

Jesus spoke about things that were fundamental to the human experience. He talked about money, stress, health, anxiety, eating, sleeping, having parties, and getting married. He talked about joy and anxiety. He talked about what it feels like to lose something and what it feels like to find it again.

One story of Jesus involves a hundred sheep and one that goes missing.

Unless you grew up in the country, you probably have never dealt with a lost sheep or even know much about sheep. In fact, sheep are not particularly intelligent animals. They are rather easy to lose because they tend to wander off. In his story, Jesus says a good shepherd values each sheep so much that if one wanders off he will go and search for it, even if this means leaving the other ninety-nine behind to find it. This is a great story about seeking out the last, lost, and least. That is what Jesus does. He seeks the one.

What is it about the one sheep that is so special? What makes it worth risking losing the other ninety-nine to go find it?

Growing up Catholic, I heard that story often. I thought how nice it is that Jesus goes after the lost, those who are "outside the flock." Surely that wasn't me. I was a cradle Catholic, firmly entrenched in the ninety-nine.

The story of the lost sheep had a subtle effect on me, as subtle as my repeated touching of my wedding ring. The effect was the thought, *I'm not that special to Jesus because I'm already "in."* I am one of the crowd. Not unique, not special, and worth leaving behind. My story is done and boring. What more is there to know or do?

Ultimately, Jesus' story of the ninety-nine and the one is about becoming lost and being found. It is about a relationship with Jesus that is real and dynamic. Each of us is "the one" Jesus is pursuing because each of us is unique and unrepeatable. We are worth seeking out. Even when we feel like we are "in," Jesus always invites us to know him more. We are the ninety-nine; we do not simply stay behind while Jesus goes out to find his lost sheep, we go out and search with him.

There are many like me—cradle Catholics and converts alike—who see themselves as part of the ninety-nine and forget they are still loved and pursued by the Good Shepherd. We should not see ourselves as valued by Jesus because we are part of his flock, the Church; we are valued as much as the one.

This book is for both the ninety-nine and the one. It is about being lost and being found—and then seeking more. It is about our relationship with Jesus and re-engaging who Jesus is, ultimately asking, "Do I believe Jesus makes a difference in my life? If so, how do I live this difference and share it?"

As you read this book, see yourself as the "one." Re-imagine your faith and relationship with Jesus. Shake yourself out of a collective mentality. Discover how your unique story ties into a Jesus' story for you. Listen for his voice as your shepherd—for he is seeking you always!

> This book is about being lost and being found—and then seeking more.

Discussion Questions ━━━━━━━━━━━━━━

1. Do you see yourself as one of the "ninety-nine"? That is, as part of Jesus' flock, close to him, following him daily, ready to hear his voice? Or do you see yourself more as the "one" who has wandered away from the Lord?

2. On a scale of one to ten, how would you rate the strength of your relationship with God at present? (One being "very weak," ten being "very strong.")

3. What would need to change for your relationship with God to deepen? Come up with three concrete ideas.

1

The Really Important Things in Life

T here was a collective and discernible gasp of horror. An usher rushed toward the sanctuary. An elderly woman in the front pew shrieked. I even heard shocked and nervous laughter echo off the tile floors. Embers and ash covered the sanctuary, and sparks flew through the air of my large suburban parish church. The priest laid dazed and confused as the incense wafted up into the heavens and there I stood, nine years old and quite embarrassed, with the thurible (i.e., the incense vessel) still swinging from the chain in my hand.

Now, I was a seasoned pro as an altar server. When lofting the crucifix for the entrance procession, I was like a finely tuned pace car, leading in the younger servers and the priest. When I was carrying a processional candle, I never allowed it to be extinguished or drip wax; leaning candles and dripping wax were for rookies. My brothers, sitting in the fifth pew on the left, tried to make me laugh as I passed them, but I never so much as cracked a smile. I was laser-focused, well-trained, and ready to serve. Until that one, fateful Sunday.

The deacon who was scheduled for that Mass—and would have been responsible for performing all incensing duties—had called in sick. So I needed to fill in. I had seen it done many times before by a deacon or priest. Nervous yet confident, I was swinging the incense to keep it smoking. This was my big break!

The Scripture readings and homily were over, and we had arrived at the part of the Mass where the priest incenses the altar. So I handed the thurible to Father John, who performed his duties. Then, the customary handoff occurred, where (usually) the deacon blesses and incenses the bowing priest.

As I said, I had seen this done before, but seeing something done and doing it are two different things. Not realizing Father was ready for the blessing, my timing was off. He bowed at the exact moment I was swinging the thurible upward—and "WHAM!"—he got a blazing thurible right to his forehead.

He fell and landed on his back, dazed and confused. The congregation (even those half asleep) recoiled in audible horror. I stood there, gaping in disbelief, my perfect altar serving record on the line and my pastor likely headed to short-term disability. David took out Goliath with a slingshot, but I had taken out Father John with a thurible.

> David took out Goliath with a slingshot, but I had taken out Father John with a thurible.

Two extraordinary ministers quickly rushed to the sanctuary to help Father to his feet. For two minutes that felt like an eternity, every eye in the congregation was on me. Some were no doubt angered by my seemingly abusive gaff, while others were amused, hiding their laughter behind hymnals and bulletins for fear of seeming irreverent. A bit later, I sure was grateful when Father John offered me the sign of peace, saying, "Next time, Mark, let's skip the incense." As he said these words, he smirked, the red wound still pulsating upon his furled brow. He was a good priest.

THOSE "CRAZY" CATHOLICS

Perhaps, like me, you are a cradle Catholic. If so, you may have been forced to don parochial school plaid or grew up with a rosary hanging on the rearview mirror of the family minivan.

Filet-o-Fish Fridays were probably a Lenten tradition. You might have experienced anxiety at your first confession, when you confessed actions you weren't even sure were sins and maybe weren't even that sorry for! You might remember the consequences (i.e., punishments) imposed by your parents if you misbehaved with your siblings during Mass.

One of six kids, our Sunday mornings were not all that peaceful. Just getting to Mass on time was like participating in the running of the bulls, with wrestling siblings and wrinkled Sunday best clothes, all crammed into the family car. I heard the name of God invoked twice as much by my father as he raced through traffic on the way to church than I ever heard from Father in the sanctuary. Mass began at 10 AM sharp and ended at 11 AM dull. The only thing in God's creation that caused me to pay any attention to what was going on was the promise of a chocolate doughnut from the Knights of Columbus table immediately after Mass.

Then again, maybe you were not raised Catholic or took a detour along the way. Maybe you left the Church to find God elsewhere. Perhaps you were not raised in any church and are not even on the market for religion or a relationship with God.

That was the situation with my buddy Mike. Unbaptized and growing up without any faith background to speak of, he had never darkened the door of a church in his life. I invited him to Mass our freshman year of college, and afterward I asked him what he thought. His response: "You guys sure do stand and kneel a lot."

All the music and mystery, the readings and preaching, communion and silent meditation, the hospitality (or lack thereof) of the community, and the majesty of the priesthood—

all this combined led to Mike's sole takeaway being a comment about posture. "You guys sure do stand and kneel a lot."

Happily, though, a seed was planted in Mike's heart. It led to further conversations, and he began to pepper me with questions about the "whats" and "whys" of everything we do as Catholics. Having grown up a cradle Catholic and attended Catholic school most of my life, I began to realize that many of the things that I took as commonplace were far from common to someone raised outside the Church.

After seeing the Catholic Faith from Mike's perspective, we certainly do have many practices and traditions that appear a bit odd, even crazy, without the proper understanding. At Mass, we stand, sit, kneel—then stand, kneel, and sit again. Once a year, on a certain Wednesday, we have ashes smeared upon our foreheads and spend the entire day displaying them in public. Every Friday of Lent we avoid eating meat.

We Catholics turn to saints to help intercede on our behalf. Have a problem or a physical ailment? We have a patron saint for that. Lose your keys? Go to St. Anthony of Padua. Stressed out about a test? St. Joseph of Cupertino is your guy. That spicy food from last night's dinner causing you some discomfort? Turn to St. Bonaventure, patron saint of stomach and bowel issues. We are always calling on the saints to assist us. While other churches have devotion to the saints, the Catholic Church takes it to a whole different level.

What about Mass? We gather each week on Sunday, and we start off with a hymn that few know and even fewer can sing well. Then we publicly confess that we have sinned as we beat ourselves on the chest. We listen to Bible readings about people and places we do not know with strange names. To top it all off, we have the audacity to proclaim—and believe—that bread and wine become the body and blood of Christ! To the outside observer like Mike, for instance, it can all seem a bit much.

While I have intentionally exaggerated some of these points and presented them out of context, we can see how someone not raised Catholic could be confused—and even why so many who do not have a relationship with Jesus leave. When we look at the content and not the context, it is easy to lose sight of the Church's true purpose.

THOSE "CRAZY" AMERICANS

Seemingly nonsensical traditions, however, are not exclusive to Catholics. Because our traditions are hundreds or even thousands of years old, not every Catholic has learned the "why" behind the "what." Some traditions evolved over time. Certain practices were handed on purposefully and precisely, while others in a less ritualistic way. Context always matters. Without context, a tradition's content is left to individual judgment and opinion.

Every people and culture has its own customs and quirks that appear confusing or foreign to the outside eye. Have you ever stopped to consider the random aspects of our own American cultural celebrations?

On New Year's Eve, we collectively huddle in our different time zones to ceremoniously watch an illuminated ball descend as we countdown to midnight, often singing "Auld Lang Syne," to which no one really knows all the words or even what it means. A month or so later, on a Sunday in early February, we celebrate an all-important yet unofficial holiday by gorging on food and drink to watch the Super Bowl—or at least its cutting-edge commercials. Around the same time, on the second of February, we wait anxiously to hear if a groundhog saw his shadow and thereby determine if winter will be long or short. Two weeks later, we celebrate a day that originally honored the life of a martyr who was tortured and clubbed to death—St. Valentine—by spending too much money on cards, flowers, candy, and dinners to say "I love you" to our significant other. Then, a month later we celebrate the life of a great Irish saint, Patrick (who was not even Irish), by donning fifty shades of green and drinking in excess.

On the fourth of July, we celebrate our independence from Great Britain by exploding bombs in the sky. The first Monday in September, we honor working men and women by taking the day off. Then, on Halloween, we dress our kids up in costumes and, despite having previously and repeatedly instructing them never to accept candy from strangers, we let them go door-to-door accepting candy from strangers. A few weeks later, we gather around bountiful tables to offer thanks for all our gifts and blessings, as we avoid discussing religion or politics or anything significant with our extended family because talking about any real issues—aside from football—might disrupt the fragile peace.

So we have many traditions, both holy and unholy, solemn and secular, that demonstrate both the highest and weirdest parts of our collective existence as humans. Yet the traditional things that bring us together increasingly seem to separate us in recent times.

ARE WE AT PEACE OR IN PIECES?

As the Greatest Generation continues to pass on and Baby Boomers grow older, we have seen a notable shift in our culture. Things such as religion and traditionally-held moral values have declined at a rapid rate. Generation X and Millennials, as a whole, are much less engaged with formerly common practices like weekly church attendance. Fewer young couples are getting married in the Church—or, for that matter, at all. Marriage rates are at an all-time low. As Millennials grow into young adulthood and Generation Z (also known as iGen) grow older, we are seeing more and more of them list their religious affiliation as "none" (approximately twenty-three percent in one 2015 study).

We are living in a unique time in human history and in our own country. The United States, once a majority Christian nation, founded upon Judeo-Christian principles, could now be described as "post-Christian" in its culture. How did this come to pass? The reasons are varied and complex. We are now more connected than ever via technology, yet we have never been more divided, fragmented, and disconnected. Ironically, the more wireless we become, the more difficult it becomes to truly unplug. As with past generations, we all seek meaning, freedom, acceptance, and respect, but we are seeking for these values in a screen-obsessed, virtual reality. Face-to-face interactions have become the exception rather than the rule. At one time, people got together and talked. Then they began to do most of their interacting through phone calls. Then, the phone gave way to texting and texts have devolved into trading emojis and GIFs.

Social media, which was created to help people share their lives and connect with one another, now seems to only be a source of division. Entire threads and text streams are filled with sarcastic memes, political outrage, racial division, and unfiltered rants designed to award the loudest voice or most convincing argument with praise. Lines are drawn, nerves are rattled, and life moves on until the next great outrage.

Until recently, when times became hard, people turned to religion for guidance and comfort. Now, many have begun to turn away from religion to seek comfort in self-help / spiritual movements or secular ideologies. Recent Church scandals have not helped the situation. There is now a widespread suspicion of religion in general and of the Church in particular, especially of its leaders and its teachings. Many wonder what role religion has in our high tech, Internet age. Isn't religion outdated in the modern world? How can it speak to people's needs today?

> We are now more connected than ever via technology, yet we have never been more divided.

THE ANSWER TO EVERYTHING

As Catholics, most of us are either going through the motions in our faith walk or are standing frozen, overwhelmed by life. What about you? How do you see the Church? Where do you seek your answers to life's questions? Where do you seek comfort in times of stress or anxiety, or when you face financial or health challenges? Do you look to God or the world?

What is this life all about anyway? What are we to make of it?

From beginning to end life is about one thing—love.

If you are in love, you probably understand this, at least intuitively. If you desire love, you also know this on some level. We have been created to love and to be loved. Without love, we are not really living; we are merely breathing.

Without love, we are not really living; we are merely breathing.

We do not think much about breathing. Without it we die, but when we think about it, a normal, involuntary action becomes almost forced and labored. All of a sudden, by focusing on it, breathing becomes all we think about. I bet you have become more aware of your breathing since starting this paragraph. It is truly amazing that something so simple, inhaling and exhaling, is necessary to live.

Life is fragile. Just speak with someone visiting a relative in intensive care or reeling from a miscarriage. Life is also unpredictable. Look no further than a city following a natural disaster. Tragedies bring out both the worst and best in the human spirit. Life is tough. People die. Marriages fail. Families separate. Jobs are lost. Anxiety is real.

It is no wonder that many ask, "Where are you, God? If you really love me, why don't you do something? Why don't you fix this situation? Don't you care? Didn't Jesus promise to be there for me, to walk with me, to help me carry my cross? Didn't he say, 'My yoke is easy, and my burden is light?' (Matthew 11:30). Yet, when push comes shove, I stand alone, with nothing to lighten my load."

So some cry out, "What about me, God? What about my sufferings?" In our prayer, we seek an immediate answer or antidote to our pain. We become impatient, even indignant, when the cure is not instantaneous or right on the horizon. It is as though we see God as our personal genie, who we can order to zap our cares away. If our prayers are not immediately answered in the way we want or expect, we feel somehow cheated or *unloved.* In these situations, we see silence or delay from God as akin to divine ambivalence or a lack of unconditional love. We begin to question not only our faith but also whether we can really trust God, whether he truly cares, and, possibly, whether he even exists.

As the stresses of life unfolds, we may fail to pray. In our pride, we believe we can do it on our own. We convince ourselves that, by sheer act of will, we will find our own solution, pull ourselves up by our bootstraps, put our head down, toughen up, and just get through it. We succeed only in frustrating ourselves all the more because God does not bless any plan or solution that makes us less reliant on him. Why would he? He sees the big picture, and only he knows how to bring about his plan of eternal love in our lives. Why would he encourage any self-directed plan that is based on trusting ourselves rather than him?

We might toil and suffer silently, putting on a brave face to the world, but we are slowly growing embittered inside. Or we might find a way to survive life's storms, to bear our cross with grace and see every challenge as an opportunity to grow in virtue. We call them saints.

At the end of the day, all we really want is to feel loved, heard, and noticed. We want the assurance that if there is a God, he not only hears our cries but also shows that he cares. If there is a God, we want the assurance that we matter. This is the relationship that we crave—because we have been created for it.

Having a relationship with God, then, is the very foundation and purpose of our traditions and religion. The word *religion*, in fact, finds its root in the Latin *religare,* which means "to bind" or "to be joined together." So religion is essentially about relationship. In and through religion, people come to know God and one another. Religious traditions and rituals are simply ongoing elements and customs that give lived expression, or form, to this relationship. Though somewhat of a dirty word in many circles today, religion is where we share our joys and sufferings *vertically* (with God) and *horizontally* (with our brothers and sisters in the faith). In Christian terms, religion is where the vertical and horizontal relationships intersect in the Cross of Christ.

In God, we find our true identity. Despite all our differences, backgrounds, fears, and struggles, our most innate desires are the same: to love and to be loved. Our unique situations and sufferings are all valid—and they all matter to God. To be sure, each of us has a story—and it is in the Author of Life (see Acts 3:15) that we discover that all of our stories are interconnected.

Discussion Questions

1. If you are a cradle Catholic (i.e., born and baptized into the Church as an infant), what was your experience of the Faith growing up?

2. How has your view of the Catholic Faith changed over the years?

3. In times of suffering do you feel more drawn to God or feel abandoned by him? Why?

4. Why do you think so many people today have grown weary of religion in general? Explain.

2

Everyone Has A Story

I have a story. So do you. Everyone does.

This was the caption that appeared under Daniel's picture in his high school yearbook. It was striking for anyone who knew Daniel. Around school he was an easily recognizable figure—cheering loudly at every game, laughing and yelling down the hallway, and often haggling with the dean of students over whether he needed to go to class.

Daniel, you see, had Asperger's Syndrome, so he often missed social cues and struggled to learn in certain classes—but he could give you detailed directions between any two American cities.

To many students, Daniel was little more than comic relief. He wasn't seen as a person with sensitivity or real emotions, so he was often the butt of jokes. But his yearbook quote stood as a quiet proclamation of humanity, affirming "I have a story. So do you. Everyone does."

When Daniel walked across the stage at graduation, he received a loud round of applause. His simple yearbook statement, "Everyone has a story," had caused people to stop and think. Daniel wasn't just comic relief, after all. He had a depth that few of his classmates had ever noticed before. They now viewed him differently; they finally saw him as they should have all along: as someone with inherent dignity, worth, and a story that mattered.

Everybody has a story. Often, we do not take the time to recognize the stories of others—and sometimes we forget our own.

What is your story? What circumstances in your life have made you the person you are? You might now be in a joyful season of your life, one made up of exciting moments, much laughter, and a lot of love. Perhaps you are beginning a new relationship, starting a new job or school, getting ready to welcome the birth of a new child or grandchild. In these times, the blessings can be multiple, visible, and obvious.

We do not take the time to recognize the stories of others—and sometimes we forget our own.

What if you are currently on the opposite side of joy? What if your story right now is comprised more of shadows than light? You might be in the midst of a difficult season. Maybe you have experienced the anxiety of the doctor's office calling with test results. Maybe your heart has been broken by the loss of a loved one, maybe you are stressed about your finances, the loss of a job, the illness of a child, or simply over the grind of daily life. These anxieties are real and can leave even the strongest soul emotionally, physically, and spiritually depleted.

Perhaps, though, you do not currently find yourself on either end of the scale. You might simply be going through the motions, following your daily routine, without too many highs and lows. You do not feel particularly happy or especially sad. You just sort of ... exist. Actually, many of us just exist.

When we think about our story, we might not see it as all that interesting, especially when we compare ourselves to the stories of others. The rapid expansion and adoption of social media has given us insight into the stories of other people like never before. Suddenly, we can not only see what someone is doing on vacation but also what they are having for dinner. We can witness intimate moments with their family and see them on a night out with friends. We tweet about our friends and family on anything from politics to sports to the newest Hollywood blockbuster, in no more than 280 characters.

Technology now connects us in incredible ways, providing insight into the stories of others in ways never before possible. Through social media, we can literally look—in real time—at other's musings on the story of a particular day. When we are stressed, it is easy to compare our day to others posted online.

We need to remember that we are not seeing the whole story. Deep down, we know this. In the gentle, constant scroll of our screen lives, though, our perspective can vanish and we can begin to see things as they aren't. We become fixated on a snapshot of another's life, forming judgments and comparisons based on this limited view. With a fateful swipe or mouse click, judgment and envy can subtly creep in and take hold. In an instant, we are virtually trapped in an alternate reality of dissatisfaction.

If we are not careful, a similar mentality can creep into our faith lives. We go to Mass every Sunday, so we see ourselves as highly involved, even holy, Christians. Then we compare our spiritual practices with those of others. We think about how our grandmother prayed the Rosary every day. We see the saints depicted in the stained glass windows of our parish church and think, "Wow. They have big life stories. Mine is little by comparison. How can I possibly be like these holy men and women?"

Maybe you see yourself as the black sheep of your family, known for unconventional or unpopular life decisions that left your relatives confused, upset, or embarrassed. Perhaps you have been challenged by them for not being "Catholic enough," for not going to church regularly or for expressing views contrary to Church teaching. Maybe you simply cannot see yourself living up to the holiness of others—or, more precisely, what you perceive to be their holiness.

In both cases, the stories and situations are valid because, again, we all have a story. When we become focused on others' stories—their struggles and pain, joys and victories—we can forget our own story. We need to avoid this trap because our unique story sheds light on who we are and where we are going.

DIVINE DESIGNER

In her poem "The Dash," Linda Ellis uses the metaphor of a tombstone to shine the light on both our collective human existence and our distinctively individual stories. Ellis points out that while every tombstone is distinct in obvious ways—different names, dates for birth and death, and inscriptions—each has one feature that is common to all—the simple dash between the year of a person's birth and the year of his or her death. Within the simple dash is a life's worth of stories, of heartbreaks and joys, victories and struggles, accomplishments and failures, and moments of grace. Every person's story is unique, and everyone's journey is guided by God's plan. The Lord's words to Jeremiah apply to all of us: "Before I formed you in the womb, I knew you, and before you were born I consecrated you" (Jeremiah 1:5).

We can never really understand another's journey in life, especially the crosses he or she might be shouldering. Most of us are so focused on our own troubles that we rarely stop long enough to consider the sufferings of others. But when we do so, we discover our common humanity, with God as our common Father. Sometimes, though, in our struggles, we might feel more like spiritual orphans than the adopted sons and daughters of God.

Even if we attend Mass on Sundays, we may not see ourselves as having a part in God's story at all, much less playing a leading role. We might see ourselves as only an extra, as somewhere in the middle of the crowd. We go through the motions on Sunday, then head into the rest of the week without feeling much different.

If that is you, do not be alarmed. It's OK. We are here to help you take a step out of the weekly church routine and into something bigger—toward *Someone* bigger.

God has an important role for you to play in his story. This might never have occurred to you before. Right now, you may not even believe it. Again, that is OK. But take a moment to consider the following questions:

> *Have you ever wondered why God made you male or female?*

> *Have you ever considered why you were born in a particular time or culture? Into your specific family?*

> *Have you ever thought about how these "lines in your biography" affected your life and viewpoint even before you left the womb?*

God created you with a unique purpose that only you can fulfill. As St. John Paul II reiterated on many occasions, every human person is unrepeatable. The circumstances of your life—both those you have some control over and those that are entirely outside of your control—are what God can use to tell your story.

You may wonder, why does God care so much about me making my part in his story something incredible?

God, the Master Craftsman, created you with precision and purpose.

Because God, the Master Craftsman, created you with precision and purpose for a vocation only you can fulfill. He is the Author who wrote you into existence simply because he desired to create you. As the beautiful words of the Lord to prophet Jeremiah so movingly teach us, "Before I formed you in the womb I knew you" (Jeremiah 1:15). You are far more than an accidental clump of cells that randomly came into existence. No, you have a divine Designer who willed you to exist from all eternity and formed you with purpose, filling you with desires and a hunger that only he can fulfill. You represent the best of God, created with purpose and made for greatness. Simply put: God made you and he cares deeply about everything he has made.

CREATED WITH A PURPOSE

Have you ever built something you were proud of? It does not have to be something physical like a shelving unit or a table. It could be a business, a career, or even your family. We feel a special attachment to the things we build. Think of a young child who constructs something out of blocks or draws a picture. He is protective of his creation and wants to show it off. The joy of creating something new often drives him to want to create more.

God is the Master Builder, the Creator. He created all we see around us. From the very beginning, thousands of years before the Bible or any other sacred book was written, humans looked at the world and recognized that there was something bigger than them that made everything around them. Whether it was the beauty of a sunrise or the calm of a starry night, every people and culture recognized there was something—or, more accurately, Someone—behind it all. They saw themselves as coming from somewhere and as a part of a greater story.

At our very core, we are religious beings. God created us that way. He created us for himself. Just like the things we create bear our imprint, we bear God's unique mark. No matter how hard we try, we cannot erase this mark; our hearts will continue to seek God, whether we want to or not. The history of religion is a testimony to our innate—and irrepressible—desire for God. Even today, in an age dominated by technology, the vast majority of the world's population participates in some religious practice, either as members of a major religious group or in some other form of spirituality. The truth is everyone worships something, even if that something is themselves. We all worship something, even if it is not God (or a god).

We all direct our life toward something or someone to give our life meaning and purpose. But does this someone or something give us a meaning or purpose that endures? Or does it ultimately leave us dissatisfied and unfulfilled?

Some things simply are true. Some truths are self-evident, as the framers of the Declaration of Independence put it. We might not like these truths, and we may want to dispute them, but we cannot change them. For example, it does not matter how hard we deny gravity; if we drop something, it will still fall to the ground. It is similarly true that God created you. An extension of that reality is that he loves you, and wants a relationship with you, both now and for eternity.

The challenge here, of course, with this truth is that it is not as self-evident as gravity. It is a truth we discover through reflection and prayer. We can see it reflected in the lives of others and in our own lives. Only after time and prayerful reflection do we discover the reality of God's love in our story. Life truly is a journey. It is about asking some big questions and having the humble courage to seek honest answers. It is about each of us discerning our own unique purpose. To do that, we need to get to know the One who created us and imbued us the specific gifts and talents we possess—gifts and talents entrusted to us to fulfill our mission here on earth.

You might be skeptical about all this. Hearing that God has this purpose, this leading role for you in his divine story might make you feel a bit uncomfortable. You might prefer to stay in the background, merely as an extra. This initial discomfort is actually a good sign; we often feel uncomfortable as we grow in self-awareness. This can be the first step to something greater.

So let us end this chapter with a few foundational questions for your consideration:

- Why do you believe what you do about God?

- Would you say your general disposition toward God is "open," "closed," or "indifferent"?

- On a scale of one to ten, where would you rate yourself, currently?

Upon reflection:

- How have you experienced God in your life up to now?

- Do you believe that he loves you and has a unique plan for you?

- How could you better hear his voice and discern his will for you?

These questions are not just foundational, they are vital. They speak mercy into our past, truth into our present, and hope into our future. What we believe about God is the most important thing in life. Consider whether you have been asking the right questions up to this point in your life. Ask yourself if you are on the right path to lasting happiness.

If we want to rediscover our story, then we need to start with one of the most basic aspects of our creation—our desire.

Discussion Questions

1. What is your story? What situations, struggles, and successes have made you "you"? Consider one or two significant life experiences that helped shape you into who you are today.

2. What is the cause of your greatest stress? Explain why.

3. What is the source of your greatest joy? Explain why.

4. What would you like "written on your tombstone"? That is, what would you like to be most remembered for after you die?

The Source of Our Desire

M y heart was slowly shattering into a million pieces. I was standing in the toy aisle at the store with the cutest little three-year-old face shining back at me. My youngest daughter was clutching a mermaid toy, begging me through tear-filled eyes to buy it for her.

As a good father, not wanting to raise a spoiled child—and fully aware that we already had several dozen mermaid toys in our house—I gently said, "No, sweetie, you don't need another mermaid. I'm sorry."

It was then that the tears, merely a slowly leaking faucet prior to that point, shot forth like an exploding fire hydrant. "PPPLLLLEEEAAASSSSEEE, Daddy!" she shouted through pouting lips in a volume strong enough to be heard over Niagara Falls-like waves emanating from her eyeballs.

My fellow shoppers—those who hadn't already fled the scene in horror—would have witnessed two things: 1) a three-year-old master manipulator in action, and 2) the deep-seeded, heart-wrenching, soul-stirring power of unfulfilled desire. Desires often dictate our actions, even in adults. The desire we have for something—and the urgency we feel to attain it—is directly proportional to the value we place upon it. For example, if I offered you five dollars to run a marathon, you would likely decline. But if I offered you five *million* dollars, you would be far more likely to accept the challenge. Our desires reflect what we value, and our actions reveal how far we are willing to go to fulfill them.

We all have desires. As we grow in age and (hopefully) wisdom, our desires change. As my three-year-old daughter grew older, she transitioned from wanting mermaids to dolls, then to electronics and, finally, clothes. Similarly, as we all transition from childhood into adolescence, our biological desires grow stronger and tend to take center stage for a while. Interestingly, though, our emotional desires, while they deepen, tend to remain consistent from childhood to old age. We all seek to be loved, affirmed, and valued at every stage of life. This is true regardless of our cultural or religious background. The innate desire for love and acceptance streams through each and every one of us.

So this begs the question: Is desire—especially our desire for love, which is universal—a byproduct of our biological makeup or does it extend beyond cells and DNA to something far greater?

LIFE ... AND THE REALLY IMPORTANT THINGS

Imagine yourself inside a car that has driven into a lake and is slowly filling with water. As the water level rises, you realize your oxygen will not last much longer. At that moment your physical need is for air but your deeper emotional—and logical—desire is for what? Life.

Or, imagine traveling through a desert and running out of water. While your mind might fabricate an oasis on the horizon as a response to your body's need for water, this imagined solution to your problem flows from your innate desire to live.

At sixteen, what is the most important thing in life? How might this change between ages sixteen and, say, thirty? What about at forty-five? At sixty? On your deathbed? Would the thing you value most be different?

When we are young we desire more money or success, but when we grow old we want more time. Few people on their deathbed wish they had worked more or accumulated more money or stuff. Most wish for another day with loved ones

> Bucket lists exist because we often fail to live each day with the end in mind.

or another year to accomplish unfulfilled dreams. Bucket lists exist because we often fail to live each day with the end in mind.

What if we flipped this approach? What if we actually lived every day with our end in mind? Rather than being led by financial goals, carnal desires, or emotional stress, what if we were instead led by something less reactive? The benefits should be obvious. For example, we would not have as much holiday weight to take off come the first day of January or need to diet before swimsuit season.

What if we actually lived in a way in which our spirit led our flesh? What if we made decisions based on something more than our carnal desires and personal goals? What if our internal GPS was calibrated by the love we all desire most deeply but cannot achieve on our own?

YOUR LIFE COMPASS

Is your life focused on the temporal or the timeless? On the immediate or the eternal? Do you live each day as if it could be your last? Continually satisfying your immediate desires can lead you down the path to selfishness and egocentrism—which ends in sadness because no human being can love you perfectly and no thing on this earth can ultimately satisfy your deepest need for the eternal.

So where is your "life compass" pointing you? Where are you headed? What guiding force directs your decision making?

Merely acknowledging our deep desire for love and acceptance is not enough. We must ask where this unshakeable and consistent human desire emanates from. You may hear atheists claim that people believe in a non-existent God because they are afraid of death or because they need something outside of themselves to get through life, to feel loved—but is this true? As we will see in the next chapter, there are strong, logical arguments for the belief in God, evidence that has nothing to do with how we feel. Plus, if people wanted merely to feel loved, they could get a dog.

In the end, everyone worships something. This can be God—or it can be money, fame, success, power, political ideology, or any number of other worldly replacements for God. Some—and they are not all atheists or secularists, some who consider themselves Christians—actually "worship" themselves. It is as though their life's compass points not outward but inward—directly to the self.

This desire for worship, to believe in God or something, is innate to our human nature. It is the way God designed us. He wants us to seek him; he alone can satisfy our deepest desires for love and acceptance. If there is a God, then the worship of anything else is folly; nothing else will never satisfy. If there is no God, then desire itself is a cruel trick of biology that leaves us only wanting more.

THE UNIVERSALITY OF DESIRE

So the question remains: Is God just an invention in the minds and hearts of people who refuse to live in reality? Is eternal life just a pipe dream used to make life livable? Aren't we just soul-less organisms, no different than any other animal, randomly (though intricately) spun into existence out of sheer luck and chemical happenstance? Can the desires I hold deep within my heart be dismissed as mere biochemical reactions within my brain responding to stimuli in my environment? The evidence would suggest otherwise.

Given the universal nature of human desire across all times and cultures—particularly the desire for unconditional love and acceptance, to feel known and valued—it seems that we can confidently deduce this is not a mere product of random genetics. Perhaps we need to be humble enough to consider that our desires are rooted in a deeper source and point to something bigger than us. The great British author C.S. Lewis, while pondering the source of our human desires once wrote, "If we find ourselves with a desire that nothing in this world can satisfy, the most probable explanation is that we were made for another world."[1]

What is this "other world"? It is nothing less than eternal life with God. All of our deepest yearnings point to this reality. In fact, creation itself stirs our hearts to the eternal. The entire cosmos speaks of it, capturing our imagination as we look up into a clear night sky blanketed with stars. As St. Paul, speaking of atheists, writes to the Roman Christians, "Ever since the creation of the world his invisible nature, namely, his eternal power and deity, has been clearly perceived in the things that have been made. So they are without excuse" (Romans 1:20).

God, then, imbues us with a desire for him and surrounds us with creation, which points directly back to the Creator. Our desires always push us toward something. As Christians, we know God, as our Creator, wants us to worship him—and this worship comes in the form of a relationship. We desire a

[1]   C.S. Lewis, *Mere Christianity* (New York: HarperOne, 2015), Bk. III, chap. 10, "Hope."

relationship with God because we have been made for it. It is as natural a desire as a need to eat or quench our thirst.

In the Old Testament, when nomadic tribes and patriarchs would strike their camps and move to a new location, the first two things these desert travelers did were dig a well and build an altar. Those two actions are related symbolically: we are thirsty both physically and spiritually. The well addressed the people's physical need for water, the altar their spiritual thirst for God. Just as water satisfies the needs of the body, worshipping God fulfills our deepest emotional and spiritual desires. This is why St. Augustine teaches, "Desire only God, and your heart will be satisfied."

Why were the Israelites so aware of their need for God? Was it because, as desert wanderers, they realized their need for God's providence and protection? It was easy for them to acknowledge their lack of control over the rain and the supply of food. These ancient, pre-technological people probably found it much easier to be present to life and to life's great realities because they were not surrounded by constant distractions as we are. They viewed themselves as important characters within God's story, each with a role and purpose. So they built altars of stone with dehydrated and tired bodies after a long journey through the desert because they desired not just to breathe but to truly live and thrive.

(UN)FULFILLED DESIRES?

God needs nothing. He is eternally perfect in himself. So he did not *need* to create us; he did so out of love. So he did not give us desires simply to live in an ache and longing for what could be. Rather, he created us with desires that *only he can fulfill*. In

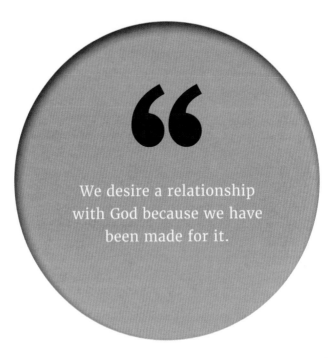

We desire a relationship with God because we have been made for it.

fact, the reason why we were created was that our greatest desires would be fulfilled.

We all have these moments of desire. Sometimes, it is for a particular food, for a big sale or a promotion at work or for that elusive playoff win by your favorite team. Other times it is far deeper, like to be reunited with a family member or return home after a long trip. There are few things more fulfilling than when I walk through the door after being away for a while and finally embrace my wife and children. I missed them more than words can express and am overjoyed when my desire to be reunited is fulfilled.

Yet we know our desires can be satisfied but never fully or in a lasting way. Many biological desires, such as those connected with eating and drinking, can be satisfied for a moment, but they are not fulfilled once-and-for-all.

This reveals a profound spiritual truth: God created our biology, so our bodies tell us something about who God is and what he has planned for us. The truth is our bodies operate in a way that always requires more, and desire signals a need for the "more" of whatever it is we need:

We get hungry and desire food, so we eat.

We get thirsty, and desire water, so we drink.

We get cold and desire warmth, so we get a blanket.

Notice all of these desires are tied to our well-being and survival. We do not just desire food because it tastes delicious; we desire it because we need to eat to survive. But we do sometimes eat a certain food simply because it tastes good, not because we are hungry. Some of our desires, then, are rooted in a psychological want rather than a biological need.

Think about things you desire that you do not have right now. You may want a new home or car. You may want to make more money or pay off some debt. What would you need to be fulfilled? Even if you get what you desire, you will still want more. You will still have desires for that which you do not have. This is the human condition.

So there is an emotional and psychological component to desire. We sometimes want things just because they make us feel good or happy, not because our body really needs them. Our desire for a certain food goes beyond hunger, and our desire for a certain drink goes beyond thirst. You might want to make more money to achieve financial stability, but what happens when you achieve this goal? Will your desire be completely satisfied? Probably not. You will look ahead at how much more money you could—or *deserve* to—have. This is the thing with desire—it can become like sugar. We consume it, are momentarily satisfied, and then crave more.

God gave us a desire for good things, including seeing beautiful art and desiring to see more, and even a desire for love and community. We are meant to be fulfilled on a level higher than mere biology. All of this points to our spiritual nature. We can never be fulfilled totally and completely on a biological level. We cannot ever be completely fulfilled on an emotional level, either. Those non-essential things that make us happy, such as success, creativity, and community, are also in constant need of renewal. They do not fulfill us all of the time. Given this fact, we can respond in two ways: 1) We can scramble endlessly looking for something that will offer us the lasting fulfillment we seek, or 2) we can accept that our desires are pointing us to something bigger than earthly fulfillment.

Many people spend their lives seeking something better, thinking that when they get what they desire, it will be enough. One person might say, "Once we move into a bigger (or better) house, we will have enough room and everything will be great." Another might think, "When I get a new car, I will be perfectly happy." Some of our desires become based on how much we can get, while others are for that one thing we believe will make us happy. We might find things like it, but then discover that they are not what we wanted and our desire remains unfulfilled. So we keep hunting for the perfect job, the perfect spouse, the perfect house, or the perfect community.

Simply put, we make fulfilling our worldly desires the end goal of our life. Our highest goal becomes trying to get enough or hunting down the unicorn. Sadly, when we do this we make those things our gods. Our desires can turn into an endless quest. When this happens, our desires have become distorted. They can even become addictive.

IDOLATRY IN THE MODERN AGE

When I was a child, I thought the first commandment, "I am the Lord your God ... you shall have no other gods before me" (see Exodus 20:2–6), which prohibits idolatry or worshipping false gods, was obsolete. After all, I didn't know anyone who had statues of other gods in their house or who worshipped some strange pantheon of gods. As a young adult, however, I came to see that I actually *did* worship other gods; they just weren't idols of stone or wood. I worshipped the gods of success, money, and comfort. I directed my time and energy toward them. They were the things I thought of when I woke up in the morning and when I went to bed at night. They were what I chased after with my whole heart, strength, and soul.

Man has been created by God as a religious being, so we all worship something. As the Bob Dylan song says, "You're gonna have to serve somebody." So why do so many find it so difficult to worship God? Why is it challenging for us to see God as our Father and make him the object of our worship, rather than some material thing or fleeting earthly desire?

There may be several answers to these questions, but let me propose a simple one: *We don't trust God*. We may trust him with certain things, but not with everything in our lives. For some reason, we do not believe he has the ability to help us with our problems or understand our situations. When it comes to our salvation, we trust God in church on Sunday morning, but not at a party on Saturday night. We trust that God hears our prayers, but not enough to trust God with our finances. So we might say that we trust God, but we hold back.

IN GOD WE (DO NOT) TRUST

So why don't we trust God? Because we are not convinced that he loves us—each of us, as a unique, unrepeatable person—and always has the best intentions for us. As Jeremiah 29:11 teaches, "For I know the plans I have for you, says the Lord, plans for welfare and not for evil, to give you a future and a hope." If we really believed that, we would have no trouble trusting God.

We cannot worship a God we do not trust. We will always wonder if God is really good and wants the best for us. When we do not worship God, we inevitably end up worshiping something, or someone, else. We have to worship God. As we have seen, it is our nature, what our desires push us toward.

To worship God is actually to engage in a proper relationship with him. If God created us out of love, then we are subject to him as our Creator and are called to love him in return. Not only that, but also he has sent his Son Jesus to teach us how to love and save us from our sin. As the first letter of John puts it, "In this is love, not that we loved God but that he loved us and sent his Son to be the expiation for our sins" (1 John 4:10). Our response to these amazing gifts should be unadulterated, loving worship.

> We can't worship a God we don't trust.

Yet we hold back.

Many Christians go to church every Sunday, yet do not have a trusting relationship with God. They feel far from him. Many have to confront the false ideas and wounds that keeps them away from God, who alone is able to fulfill their deepest desire. These wounds often relate to broken or even abusive relationships with parents or family members from an early age that lead to a pattern of distrust.

Trust is the result of knowing that *you are loved.*

Instead of experiencing unconditional loving providers and protectors, many people had parents who were flawed and broken, absent, angry or uncaring. Many people learned, from a young age, that those who were supposed to be a source of support and stability were actually untrustworthy.

This may be part of your own story. You may be calling to mind how it felt when your mom or dad walked out of your house for the last time, never to return. You may be feeling the sting of divorce or remembering a parent who spent more time with a bottle than with you.

If that is your story, while you will not be able to change the past, God has plans for your future, no matter your age. Your wounds might be difficult to look at, and it might be helpful to meet with a skilled Christian therapist to help you walk through it. The wound a parent leaves on your heart when they do not love you the way they should can have a profound impact on your life. You deserve to be healed.

Our family wounds can distort our vision of God. As a result of such wounds, many are uncomfortable—or even unable—to have a relationship with God as Father, even though this is how Jesus himself tells us to call on God. They see the inadequacy of their own fathers and superimpose this image on God the Father. Such people were never able to trust their earthly fathers, so they find it difficult to trust their heavenly Father.

If you are struggling with having a relationship with God as Father, take a step back. Seek the counsel of a holy priest or a good Catholic counselor. Remember that God transcends human fatherhood, though he is its ideal model. As St. Paul tells us, "For this reason I bow my knees before the Father, from whom every family in heaven and on earth is named" (Ephesians 3:14–15). So there are profound theological reasons for calling God "Father," following the example of Jesus himself. It is as Father that God especially wants us to trust him—to trust that he loves each of us and wants us to be in a relationship with him, both now and in eternity.

OUR DESIRES CAN BE FULFILLED, AFTER ALL

Since God gave us a desire for ultimate fulfillment in him, he must give us the means for them to be fulfilled. We must trust him. If we cannot trust God, we will never be able to give ourselves over to him; we will never be able to have a deep, loving, and lasting relationship with him.

So it comes down to this: we need to acknowledge that we have desires that point us to something more. This something more is God, but if we seek to fulfill our desires with something other than God we will be disappointed and unsuccessful. We will continually seek "the next, best thing," never really achieving what we want because our desires go on and on. We end up unsatisfied. In the end, our only alternative is to seek the fulfillment of our desires in God, as Father, trusting that he will provide what we need as we grow in our relationship with him.

All of this will strike some as too good to be true, as too hard to believe. As we move forward, then, we will pause and examine some of our core beliefs as Christians, using logic and reason along the way. We need to take both faith and reason into account as we consider what exactly we believe about God and why.

Discussion Questions ───────────────

1. What do you desire most in your life at present?

2. What do you desire most to achieve before you die? Is this the same as the answer to question one or is it different? Why do you think this is the case?

3. Consider how each of the following might currently guide your decisions. Add a percentage to each:

   Stress _____   Past sins or feeling
                               of guilt _____
   Money _____
                               God _____
   Fear _____
                               Something else _____
   The future _____

4. What earthly things can frequently direct our desires away from God?

5. Do you find the idea of God as "Father" comforting and helpful or foreign and difficult? Why?

A "Reason"able Belief in God

B

elief is a powerful thing.

A person who is truly convicted in his or her beliefs can change the world. History shows this truth in incredible examples of heroism, as people embraced ideals about freedom, equality, and justice. Unfortunately, certain beliefs are misguided or evil. When such beliefs are held and advanced by charismatic world leaders, great wars have often been the result.

One's sincere beliefs are worth fighting for.

What do you believe? What in your life is worth fighting for?

I think often about my own life and the things I believe.

For example:

I believe that ninety percent of all standing ovations are based on peer pressure.

I believe that pizza, no matter how bad, is still pretty good.

I believe that there should be a federal law outlawing the designated hitter in Major League Baseball.

I believe that the Fighting Irish of Notre Dame are the greatest college football team to follow.

I believe that family should always come first.

I believe that Jesus Christ is the Incarnate Son of God who came to save me from my sins.

Looking at that list, it is fairly easy to see that each of these beliefs has different implications. At the end of my life, my thoughts regarding pizza or the designated hitter rule will not matter much. My beliefs about the importance of Jesus and family will, though.

Each of us has a hierarchy of beliefs, whether we realize it or not, and most are not beliefs that are worth fighting for. But there are some beliefs we are passionate about, for example: we probably react strongly when a core principle of who we are is threatened.

> Each of us has a hierarchy of belief, whether we realize it or not.

Think about your hierarchy of beliefs. What beliefs do you find yourself arguing about the most?

Which would you fight to defend? Which would you die for, if you had to?

WHAT MATTERS MOST

As you examine your beliefs, you may come to see that some you fight for really are not worth it. Some you should simply let go, with the understanding that you have your view and others have theirs. Every summer, for example, baseball fans are thrown out of games over arguments with the umpire over a perceived missed call or over a fight with another fan. These diehard fans need to step back and ask themselves if jail time is really worth sucker punching an opposing fan because he does not like their team.

I have seen those kinds of fights myself—at little league baseball games. I have witnessed full-grown adults get into physical altercations over the gameplay of twelve-year olds. I have also been in situations in which a person's deepest-held religious beliefs were insulted and they sat back and said nothing.

Where on your hierarchy of beliefs is your faith? Is it worth arguing over or fighting for? You may want it to be at the top, but maybe—if you are being honest with yourself—you typically avoiding talking about your faith or confronting those who challenge it. In today's cultural climate, few would blame you for that.

No doubt that there are more people who will get into a shouting match over a missed call in a Little League game than enter into a debate about their faith.

Why? If we believe that our faith has eternal implications, isn't that something worth sharing and defending? Why do we shy away from something so important? Perhaps because we live in an increasingly secular culture, where the very subject of religion has become contentious.

THE "R" WORD

Recent studies have shown that fewer and fewer people are actually convicted of whatever religious beliefs they may have. Most religions require their followers to adopt teachings and practices that are at times challenging. If a person is not fully convicted of his or her faith, it is easy to only follow the comfortable parts of one's religion and eventually fall away completely. As we have seen, the true purpose of religion is relationship. Religion is the way in which people come to know about God and enter into a relationship with him. When this fundamental understanding of relationship is lost, everything becomes distorted.

Compounding this reality is that more people are becoming openly hostile to organized religion and even personal religious beliefs. In recent decades, several prominent atheists have openly attacked religion, stating that even personal religious belief is a threat to the happiness of all people. They see religious faith and practice as a cause of evil in the world that must be eliminated. The arguments they use can seem especially convincing if we are not convicted of our belief system. Tragically, many people have found themselves walking away from their faith after hearing some of these seemingly valid arguments.

In college, I fell headlong into these arguments. I joined an online atheist forum—the digital version of walking into the proverbial lion's den. I boldly posted an article I wrote entitled "A Christian's Reason to Believe," and the response was immediate. The comments continued to be posted for more than a year. Hundreds of self-described agnostics and atheists engaged in a dialogue based on the assertions of my article. Not surprisingly, arguments against God, religion, or having faith in anything. The only reality, they maintain, is that which we can observe and measure.

The core of their argument: It is unreasonable and even silly to believe in a higher power, let alone a personal God who is interested in the lives of every person who has ever existed, exists currently, or will exist. For an atheist, all of us are faced with a rather stark choice—either believe in God, thereby living in a prescientific dark age or leave superstition behind and embrace the enlightened teachings of science, thereby rejecting the existence of God.

If we have never considered *why* we believe what we believe about God, Jesus, the Church, or our faith, the choice presented by atheism can shake us. We do not want people to think we are ignorant or stupid. This is nothing to be ashamed of because many people grow up as Catholics but never face the tough questions. Some people fear that asking these questions will cause their entire belief system to crumble, so they simply avoid them. Others ask the hard questions but do not know where to turn for answers. Some questions require a bit of a journey to answer.

THE PATH TO TRUTH

So let us consider the most fundamental, difficult question of all: Is it reasonable to believe in God who is personally interested in us?

This question is not new. For thousands of years, some of the world's brightest philosophers and theologians—as well as poets and artists—have asked this question. Interestingly, all of them reached a similar conclusion: not only is belief in God reasonable, it is more reasonable than the alternative.

Before we dive into how we can use reason to prove the existence of God, we need to grasp the nature of science, reason, philosophy, and faith. All four disciplines are distinct but interwoven. Each have a distinct role to play in our understanding of reality.

As it turns out, science and faith are not mutually exclusive. Each has its proper place. Science, of course, is useful— essential even—for describing how physical realities work. It is adept at answering the "how" questions. As such, science is responsible for creating the technology that makes modern life possible. When an aeronautical engineer designs an airplane, for example, you want him to use science rather than faith in his engineering work. His faith actually has very little to do with the airworthiness of his jet design. Imagine if he was present to greet you as you boarded the plane he designed, and you asked him how he went about it. You certainly would not want to hear him say, "Well, when we put this plane together, we didn't really worry about the details. We just believed it would fly. So we threw out the plans and took it all on faith." At that point, it might be smart to get off that plane as quickly as possible, or begin drafting your will.

Nor are modern medicine, transportation, and communication, created by faith; they are developed through research and testing, using the tools of science. In fact, when we utilize science to help make our world better to improve the overall well-being of humanity, we are using science the way that God intended it to work. This is important for us to keep in mind.

If we believe that God created all things from nothing, we must also believe that God created them in a way that makes sense. God is the Master Designer; he created a universe that operates according to established laws and functions in an orderly way that we can (at least partially) understand. There is not chaos when God creates. God makes order.

The creation narrative at the beginning of the Bible is well known. According to the book of Genesis, God created the world in six days and rested on the seventh. From the perspective of modern science, this claim would be considered a fairy tale. If we are reading it as science then, yes, we should discount it. This narrative in Genesis is not intended to present a scientific view of the origins of the earth. It is not interested in telling us about *how* the universe came about but *why*. When we look at the Genesis creation account from a theological standpoint— that is, by asking, "What does this tell us about God?"—we reach an interesting conclusion.

We see that God created in an orderly way, with ever increasing complexity. For example, animals are necessarily created after there is land to walk on and water to drink—and the land and water are created only after there is a place for both to exist, i.e., the earth. Over the six days of creation, then, there is a logical progression from chaos to order. The message is clear: God creates order out of chaos.

PUTTING FAITH IN REASON

Scientific inquiry, if properly understood, does not actually point us away from a creator and toward nothingness; rather, it reminds us that the complexity in the world can only come from the mind of something infinitely more complex. Science, in its proper form, should point us *toward* God, not away from him.

This is evidenced by the many key scientific discoveries made by Catholics, particularly priests and monks. Here, we can think of Georges Lamaitre (1894–1966), a Belgian Catholic priest and astronomer, who developed what is commonly known as the Big Bang theory—a view of the origin of the universe that is universally affirmed by astrophysicists today. We can also mention Gregor Mendel (1822–1894), an Augustinian friar and biologist, who is considered by many to be the father of modern genetics. Or Italian priest and Guiseppe Mercalli (1850–1914), who developed the scale used to measure the intensity of earthquakes.[1]

While the Church (and religion in general) has been accused of being "anti-science," the Vatican actually has an entire department devoted to scientific research—the Pontifical

---

[1]   These are only three examples of many. Research the lives of St. Albert the Great (1200–1280), Fr. Giovanni Riccioli (1598–1671), Bishop Nicolas Steno (1638–1686), Fr. Julius Nieuwland (1878–1936), and Fr. William of Ockham (1287–1347) for further evidence of the Church's invaluable contribution to the sciences.

Academy of Sciences, which was established by Pope Pius XI in 1936. While some religions may shun modern science, the Catholic Church is not one of them, especially in modern times. Several popes over the past couple of centuries have written about the role science plays in our knowledge of creation, and a foundational part of Catholic teaching revolves around the importance of scientific inquiry.

The limits of scientific inquiry need to be respected, however. Science, for example, can neither prove nor disprove the existence of God. Why? Because proving God's existence—that is, of an eternal being who exists outside of space and time—is entirely beyond the scientific method, which relies on observation and measurement. The insights of modern science do provide evidence that there is something behind the complexity of the universe, but science itself has nothing to say on God. This question lies squarely in the realm of reason and faith.

Reason has been given to us by God so that we may understand him in a deeper way. God does not want us to be unreasonable in our faith, nor does he want us to have a simplistic, childish faith. In Matthew 18:3, Jesus calls us to be *child-like* in our faith. We are called to seek understanding for the big questions of life, similar to the way children asks their parents, "Why?" and trust that their parents will give them an answer they can understand.

As we grow, we naturally are faced with seeking answers to life's big questions. Children are not yet ready to understand complex math problems but become equipped to do so as they mature. Similarly, as adults, we have a duty to understand the "why"s behind what we believe about God. When we were younger, it was sufficient to say, "We know God exists because we can feel His love," but as we get older we need to build on that answer.

"PROVING" THE EXISTENCE OF GOD

Over the course of the centuries, several philosophers have offered various proofs for God's existence. It is important to note, however, that these arguments do not definitely *prove* God exists; they merely offer clear logical and rational evidence for his existence. These arguments are not akin to mathematical proofs, then. Rather, these are simply reasonable arguments in favor of belief in a higher power, an "uncreated Creator" or "unmoved Mover"—a first cause of everything that is.

The most famous classical proofs for God's existence were devised by the thirteenth-century Italian Dominican theologian St. Thomas Aquinas (1225–1274). Even St. Thomas recognized that these were not proofs in the strictest sense; he does not even call them that in his writing. Rather, he calls them the "Five Ways"—indicating from the very start that reason cannot replace faith; it can merely support and strengthen it.

These five ways are rooted in arguments from: 1) motion, 2) efficient cause, 3) possibility and necessity, 4) gradation, and 5) governance. St. Thomas presents these arguments in full in his *Summa Theologica*, but for now we will summarize each of these five ways. From them, we can see that not only is it reasonable to believe in God, but also far more unreasonable not to believe.

 1   Argument from Motion

Here, we begin with the rather self-evident observation that "things move."

If you doubt this, just pick up something and throw it across the room. (Preferably, something not too heavy, something that will not put a hole in the wall or knock down the family picture.) In doing this, you will observe one of the fundamental laws of physics—namely, an object at rest tends to stay at rest unless acted on by an outside force. The outside force in this case was you—specifically, your hand and arm. Interestingly, though, your body—the force moving the object—also needed to be moved before the object could be thrown.

No object can "move itself"; something needs to move it. The object in question had the potential to move though, and this potential for motion became actualized when you threw it.

Before that, of course, your hand and arm had the potential to move; they moved when electrical impulses from your brain, acting through your nervous system, moved the muscles in your arm, hand, and fingers.

You get the idea. There is always some other force at work prior to movement that takes something from the potential to move to actually moving. Every movement, then, has a mover. Logically, there must be a first mover at the very beginning of all motion—an unmoved Mover. We call this unmoved Mover God.

Argument from Causality

Another not-so-startling reality we can observe in everyday life is that every effect has a cause. In other words, everything that happens must be caused by something else. An apple falls to the ground due to gravity—i.e., gravity causes it to fall.

For all those causes—something caused them, too. So the line of causes goes on and on and on.

Accordingly to St. Thomas, the line of causality cannot be endless; it must have a definite beginning. All causes ultimately need to be rooted in a first Cause, an uncaused Cause—God.

3   Argument from Possibility and Necessity

If a child points to a tree and asks you where it came from, you would respond that it came from a seed. If he or she then asks, "Well, where did that seed come from?" You would say, "From another tree." Then, the child might ask you how a tree grows. You might respond that the soil in which it is planted helps it to grow by providing water and nutrients—and that the light from the sun provides its leaves with the energy (via photosynthesis) it needs. The soil and sun also came from other preexisting components, which in turn come from others, and so on.

A seed has all the potential to become a tree. Although it needs other things—soil, light, water—for it to grow. These things that a seed needs to reach its potential—a tree—also need other components to make them up. So everything that exists is dependent upon other things for its existence.

St. Thomas' third way of knowing that God exists, then, is the argument from "possibility and necessity." Simply put: things exist, but everything that exists comes into being from something else. But this chain cannot go on forever; there has to be a starting point—a starting "necessity," a "necessary Being"—from which all other possibilities can proceed. We call this starting point, this necessary being, God.

4   Argument from Gradation

What is the hottest thing you can think of? How do you know it is the hottest? You do this by comparing it other hot things—by using some sort of scale, a system of measuring temperature (either Celsius or Fahrenheit). We use the scale, then, as a point of reference to decide which things are hotter (or colder or heavier or larger) than others. You could also think of the best movie you have ever seen, and this becomes the top of your scale against which every other movie is measured.

St. Thomas Aquinas uses this idea of "gradation" when he speaks about God. Certain things are hard to measure against an objective scale—goodness and beauty, for example. If we recognize that goodness and beauty exist, how do we determine what is most beautiful or most good? There must be a standard we can use to measure them. There has to be something that is "most beautiful" or "perfect goodness" in itself. Aquinas says that this perfect beauty or goodness— the perfection of all things, in fact—is God himself.

5 Argument from Design

The fifth way that St. Thomas offers comes from the design of things, or what he calls unintelligent bodies. When we look at the world around us, we observe that everything works toward an end, a goal. Everything seems to be ordered and designed for a specific purpose. This purpose or end, however, is not determined by things themselves. A tree does not decide to be a tree, or what it means to be a tree, or what "tree-ness" is. This is obvious, you might say trees do not have brains or self-awareness. Human beings, some would say, are different: we can determine what we want to be, but is this really true? Do any of us decide our nature, either as a human in general or the unique person we are? Do we have any role in writing the blueprint for who we are, designing ourselves with our particular appearance or intelligence or talents?

Another way to look at this argument is to think of a complex item, such as a smartphone. If you were an intelligent being from another planet and came across this seemingly odd device, you wouldn't assume that the materials from which it is made simply came together spontaneously; it obviously has some purposeful design, and a design needs a designer. The same is true for our world; when we see how everything operates we look for a higher intelligence that designed it, and we call this higher intelligence God.

DOES ANY OF THIS REALLY MATTER?

These five ways of St. Thomas Aquinas are not the only proof for God's existence that have been offered by philosophers. This question has been debated over the centuries and various arguments have been proposed. Some are simple, others are incredibly complex.

In the end, though, does any of this matter?

I asked myself this question in college. I was studying religion, and as part of my course of study, I learned about the various world religions. This was the first time I really considered what others believed. While I had always believed in a higher power, I had to wrestle with the question how much this higher power mattered to my life. After all, there are major implications to believing in an impersonal higher power versus a personal God who loves me and makes demands on my life.

So the various philosophical proofs for God's existence provide compelling, logical reasons to believe in an intelligent creator, but does this creator really intervene in daily life. Or is he (or it) merely an impersonal force that set the world in motion and just let things run, without any involvement in the daily

A design
needs a designer.

> God doesn't need us; he *wants* us.

lives of human beings? These are vital questions that simply proving the existence of God cannot answer.

If an all-powerful God created the universe and, consequently the people in it, one has to ask, why? Did God *need* to create the universe? Was something lacking him? After creating, could this God then simply ignore his own intelligently designed creation? If the universe was created by God according to his design, should we not seek to understand this design and live according to his plan?

Of course, we could just walk away from these questions. We could simply pretend that they do not matter. If God created the universe not out of need but out of love, then we have a great value. God does not need us; he wants us. If God did in fact create the universe with a design in mind, then there is a best way to live and for the world to work. Finally, if that God in fact does will our best, which would make sense given that God created us in the first place, then it would make sense for God to reveal this plan to us, to show us how it all works.

A GOD WHO COMES CLOSE

The big question, then, of whether God exists can be answered with a resounding, "Yes, it is reasonable to believe that God exists. In fact, it is more reasonable to believe in God than not to." But is this God a distant, uncaring, impersonal force or is he a loving, personal Father who seeks a relationship with each of us?

Nearly all ancient cultures believed in not one but in many gods. They were polytheists. To these peoples, such as the Sumerians, Assyrians, and Egyptians, this made perfect sense. Just as there was a diversity of roles in society, there must be different gods with various roles in the celestial world. Each god had a different character and function.

What makes the religion of the ancient Israelites unique, however, is its radical monotheism. Instead of several gods, they believed in only one. Not only that, but also they knew this God in a real and personal way. This God even went so far as to speak to them his name (see Exodus 3:13–15). In the ancient world, names revealed a person's nature.

The Israelites come to know that God is not just some distant Creator, one who spoke creation into existence without any thought, plan, or continuing interest in it. In the first chapter of Genesis, we can see the form and function God gave his creation. Then, in Genesis, chapter two, we see a God who "draws near" by creating man and woman in his image and likeness. We see a God who is "hands-on," walking with them in the garden, calling them by name. We see a God who wants to be a Father to his children, not a master to his slaves. God draws near to his people.

The history of the Israelites recorded in the Old Testament is a love story. It is about a people who are special to God—the one and only God—and who will know him in a unique way. God had big plans for the Israelites, though. It was through them that his plan of salvation would be revealed to the world. To achieve this plan, God enters into a special agreement—a covenant—with the Israelites, promising them his providence and protection in return for their obedience and worship of him.

RITUAL V. RELATIONSHIP

The Israelites lived out their relationship with God through various religious practices. They interacted with God through worship and demonstrated their relationship with him through their obedience to the rituals he had prescribed. God doesn't just want us to know his commandments like the back of our hand; he wants us to follow them with the fullness of our hearts.

As we have seen, the word *religion* has a negative connotation to many today. Some even claim that religion takes the place of a real relationship. If a person seeks to be religious by simply going through the motions and doing the right things while having no real, personal relationship with God then, yes, religion can be a bad thing. Jesus addressed this dark side of religious practice when he confronted the Pharisees for having hearts "far from God" and teaching "precepts of men" (see Mark 7:6–7).

So God wants a relationship with us, and it is our relationship with him that is celebrated in our religious rituals. It is a lot like a marriage—which is the image God uses more than any other in the Bible to explain his immeasurable love for us and to show the deep, personal relationship he desires with us. When a man and woman love and sacrifice for each other, this love blossoms in certain behaviors, practices, and rituals.

Rituals are an important part of relationships, especially in marriage. My wife and I feel the strain when we get off our schedule of having a weekly date night. Every day when I get home from work, we have a ritual where we each download everything from our day. When this sharing is interrupted, usually by our kids, the entire house becomes tense because we have not been able to connect fully with one another at the end of the day. Rituals are a vital part of relationships.

That said, rituals cannot *become* the relationship, or take the place of a true relationship. If the rituals my wife and I practice are not backed by authentic love, by an authentic connection, they can become empty. They become a going through the motions. At the end of the day, I would just be reporting what happened to me and my wife would do the same, without really caring about what I am sharing or how I am delivering it. This important connection would be reduced to rambling—I would just be I putting in my time with our daily download.

On the other hand, if my wife and I suddenly disregarded all of our rituals, we could easily get caught up by our parenting and our work and not even realize we were no longer making time for each other as spouses.

If our God was simply a remote and impersonal force, then we could be just purely religious—we could simply practice rituals and do things to please him. But our God is personal, so we need to seek a relationship with him. He designed us for a relationship with him! As St. Augustine so famously teaches in his *Confessions*, "You have made us for yourself, O Lord, and our hearts are restless unless they rest in you."

Still, an unseen God can seem remote. Our religious practices may at times feel one-sided. God established a covenant relationship with his people, the Israelites, and gave them rituals because he had something big in mind. He was preparing the stage for the next act in his relationship with us—sending a savior in the person of his Son, Jesus. The un-knowable God was about to make himself known in a whole new way.

If we affirm that there is a God—and that he is a personal God who calls us to a relationship with him—then we need to take the next step and ask, "Just how personal does this God get?"

As personal as flesh and blood.

Discussion Questions ───────────────

1. What do you believe are the five most important things in life?

2. Does your daily schedule—your daily rhythm— reflect your previous answer? Why or why not?

3. Why do you believe in God? If you struggle to believe in God, what is your biggest challenge?

4. Do you accept the claim that God's existence can be demonstrated by reason alone, that is, without faith? Why or why not?

5. The assertion that "God does not need us; he wants us" can be difficult for many to accept. Do you believe this? Why or why not?

5

Putting Jesus to the Test

Several years ago, I came across an article that really stuck with me. It describes the life of an obscure and unimpressive man—from a worldly perspective, that is—who goes on to have the most profound impact of any individual who ever lived.

One Solitary Life

He was born in an obscure village, the child of a peasant woman. He grew up in still another village, where he worked in a carpenter's shop until he was thirty. Then for three years he was an itinerant preacher.

He never wrote a book. He never held an office. He never had a family or owned a house. He did not go to college. He never visited a big city. He never traveled two hundred miles from the place where he was born. He did none of the things one usually associates with greatness. He had no credentials but himself.

He was only thirty-three when the tide of public opinion turned against him. His friends ran away. He was turned over to his enemies and went through the mockery of a trial. He was nailed to a [stake] between two thieves. While he was dying, his executioners gambled for his clothing, the only property he had on earth. When he was dead, he was laid in a borrowed grave through the pity of a friend.

Twenty centuries have come and gone, and today he remains the central figure of the human race, and the leader of mankind's progress. All the armies that ever marched, all the navies that ever sailed, all the parliaments that ever sat, all the kings that ever reigned, put together, have not affected the life of man on this planet so much as that one solitary life.[1]

---

[1]   Attributed to James Allen Francis (1864-1928)

The life of Jesus is unmistakably the most influential of any life ever lived. No one person has ever affected human culture, art, religion, politics, philosophy, moral theology, virtue, education or familial structure the way Jesus did. But does a historical resume make him the Son of God?

HIGHER EDUCATION?

During my first semester in college, I was both excited and nervous when I walked into my first college course on the New Testament. Since I was attending a state university, the fact that there was a course offered on the New Testament was a welcome surprise. While many of my friends who attended Catholic colleges had religion courses readily available, my options were much more limited. So when I saw this course was available in the fall semester, I immediately signed up.

The professor entered the room and greeted us with the following words: "I want to make one thing clear from the start. This is not a Bible study. This is about history and the historical Jesus. Jesus existed, but he was not God." A few students gasped at these rather surprising, extraordinary remarks.

In the coming weeks, some students argued, walked out of class, and dropped the course as the teacher approached the New Testament as I never experienced before. As the instructor promised, it certainly was *not* a Bible study. Instead, it was focused on looking historically at some of the most influential documents ever written.

As the course neared its completion, though, I reached a different conclusion from my professor. After hearing the historical evidence, learning how and why the Gospels were written, and discovering that non-Christian sources all attested to the existence of Jesus, I could only believe that

Jesus was, in fact, the Messiah, the Son of God. There was no other explanation for the evidence presented. No way to explain away the fact that Jesus' life and teachings had stood the tests of time, persecution, and scandal.

Whether or not one believes that Jesus was divine, simply a good man who taught an interesting philosophy, or is a myth, there is universal agreement on one point:

There is no other person who has had as much impact on history.

Jesus is referenced within both Christian and non-Christian writings (e.g., Josephus, Tacitus, and the Babylonian Talmud, to name a few). A whole movement of people sprang up, seemingly out of nowhere, who enthusiastically followed his teachings, many to the point of extreme suffering and death. So there are three main issues we need to contend with:

1. Did Jesus exist as an historical person? If not, then the entire "Jesus story" was just made up, and we can put his life and teachings on the same level as any great work of literature—worth reading and reflecting on, but certainly not committing one's life to or dying for.

2. If Jesus existed, then who was he? Was he who he claimed to be—namely, the Son of God? This would make him equal to God himself. So he was either a manipulative liar, completely delusional and insane, or telling the truth.

3. If Jesus existed and truly was the Son of God, what does this mean for us and the way we live our lives?

We need to break these three things down because there can be a tendency to take each of them for granted, especially if we were raised as Christians. We may simply believe that Jesus existed, but may never have considered the evidence. The same holds true for Jesus' claims about being God and, consequently, how we should live our lives.

THE HISTORICAL JESUS

How do we know George Washington existed? Well, the first president's face adorns the one dollar bill, his name is on many monuments—and cities, universities, and organizations have been named after him. His life is legendary and, by many accounts, was somewhat mythic even during his lifetime.

Why do you trust that he existed, though? Probably because somebody, a teacher maybe, told you when you were young. How did he or she know? From reading about Washington in a history book. Was that book telling the truth? Maybe. Perhaps it recounted the historical details correctly but likely with a particular slant. There may have been bias in the telling of Washington's life.

Still, you believe George Washington existed, but you are trusting a few (actually a lot) of other people to communicate this information to you. There is compelling evidence to believe in his existence. With the sheer volumes of information we have about his life, one could reasonably say that George Washington was a real person, and we can trust the historical record about his life.

History is important, but equally important is understanding how history is recorded and passed down. People that argue Jesus never existed—and there are very few of them actually, with no reputable historian among them—question the historical accuracy of the accounts of his life and deeds.

On the surface, objections to Jesus' existence as a purely historical figure might seem reasonable. Who had the most to gain from manufacturing the story of Jesus? Clearly his followers, who may have been seeking separation from the Jewish community and a reason to take control. It could have even been someone within the Roman government of Judea that created the narrative of a passive Jewish leader who told people to pay taxes to the government, turn the other cheek, and be obedient to local authorities while painting the current Jewish leadership (the Sanhedrin, composed of Sadducees and Pharisees) in a poor light. Maybe Jesus was simply a well-crafted piece of propaganda.

NO SANTA, NO GOD?

I remember when I found out that Santa Claus didn't exist. I was eight. I discovered evidence that was left over from Christmas shopping my parents did under the guise of Santa, and all of the puzzle pieces fell into place. I was upset; my parents had lied to me. I ran through the house to find my mother and accused her of her lies, then ran to her bedroom and threw myself on the bed, crying.

After a few minutes she came into the room to console me and confirmed that Santa Claus did not, in fact, exist. Neither did the Easter Bunny, the tooth fairy, or any of the other characters my parents told me about growing up. Painful realizations set in, along with some questions. First, what did my parents do with all those teeth (I found out later my mom kept most of them), and second, what else were my parents lying about?

I looked at my mom through tears and became angry as she finished telling me that all my childhood saviors were fake. So then I asked, "So what, God's not real, either?"

She paused for a moment. Suddenly, this conversation about Santa Claus took a turn she didn't expect. As a child, I made the jump from all the stories my parents told about Santa Claus and immediately equated them to what they told me about the Faith. It all seemed to fit: God wanted me to be good or I would go to hell; Santa wanted me to be good or I wouldn't get presents. I couldn't see either one and needed to believe in other people telling me they existed. When I questioned the reality of either, I was told to just believe. It didn't seem like a big jump.

Many atheists use the same argument to dissuade people from belief in God. They look at other places where people believed in something that turned out to be false like Santa Claus, and they draw the parallels. This simple argument can seem persuasive, especially in a world devoid of fact checking and where people get their current news from a meme. When we dig deeper, though, we can come to a very reasonable answer that Jesus not only existed, but also his existence had a profound impact on the world in which he lived. Santa Claus he wasn't.

Think about the people who were there, especially the disciples. If Jesus' followers simply manufactured the whole "Jesus" thing to gain power, authority, and money, it was a terrible plan. It did not turn out so well for them, did it? They were persecuted and most were killed, as attested to by several non-Christian sources. Until the fourth century in the Roman Empire, the practice of Christianity was outlawed and Christians were regularly executed by the government. The Christian religion was not protected because it opposed the gods of Rome and refused to pay taxes that supported the worship of false gods. Incredibly, though, Christianity persisted and even won converts. Ancient writers spoke about Christians and how much they loved each other, as well as their joy, but those statements were not written in reference to any great parties the Christians were throwing. They were written upon reflecting on how Christians appeared before they were killed in the Coliseum. People were deciding to become Christians as they witnessed Christians being martyred. Think about that. The manner in which early Christians faced persecution and death is what convinced people to join this persecuted movement.

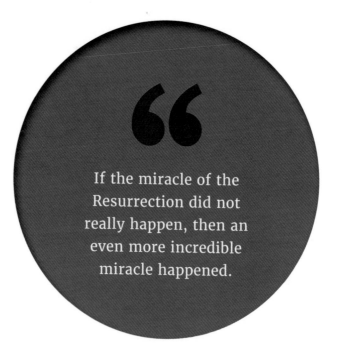

If the miracle of the Resurrection did not really happen, then an even more incredible miracle happened.

Would you die for belief in Santa Claus?

There is something at work here. The conviction of the early disciples of Jesus was profound. They knew the "Jesus story" was true because they knew Jesus, and they passed along their zeal to subsequent generations of his followers. People do not die for lies. As noted Catholic philosopher and author Peter Kreeft puts it, "If the miracle of the Resurrection did not really happen, then an even more incredible miracle happened: twelve Jewish fisherman invented the world's biggest lie for no reason at all and died for it with joy, as did millions of others."[2]

If the Jesus movement was really about money, power, or fame, the disciples might have endured a certain amount of suffering but they would have turned back in the face of death. Wealth and power is no good once you are dead. In the face of persecution, the early Church would have surely abandoned belief in Jesus. Better to save one's life than die for a lie. But die they did, a lot of them.

There were other revolutionary movements at the time of Jesus. There were groups of people that believed in a big cause. They all disappeared. They were persecuted by the authorities or people just lost interest and walked away. The followers of Jesus knew something and had experienced something. They had experienced God through Jesus, and that reality was worth dying for.

THIS MAN CALLED JESUS

What was it about Jesus that was so captivating? His message was certainly countercultural, including seeking and serving

2   Peter Kreeft, *Fundamentals of the Faith: Essays in Christian Apologetics* (San Francisco: Ignatius Press, 1988), xxx

the last, lost, and least. But think about his claims—Jesus said he was God. That is pretty bold.

Can you imagine if a man came to your town or city teaching in the street and telling everyone that he was divine? You would think he was crazy. And with good reason. In college, people would show up on campus to talk about whatever their particular cause was. Students and faculty would walk by and pay no attention at all. These people gained few followers.

If someone showed up to on a college campus claiming to be God, he or she would be escorted off the property by police. How much credibility would you give to someone who said, "I am the way, the truth, and the life"?

That is exactly what Jesus claimed. He is unique in this assertion about himself, but not because of the content. Many others throughout history claimed to be divine. He is unique because none of the founders of the world's other major religious systems—Buddha, Mohammad, Confucius—claimed to be God. They simply claimed to speak on behalf of God or to share a special kind of knowledge to help us understand the world. They never claimed divinity. Other major religious leaders didn't actually claim to be God.

Jesus did, and unlike the many other people who claimed to be divine, the religion of Jesus had lasted.

The great Christian author C.S. Lewis (1898–1963) put forward the idea that Jesus could only be one of three things, based on his claims: a liar, a lunatic, or the Lord (i.e., he was what he claimed to be—the Son of God). His reasoning is simple: If Jesus claimed to be God but knew he wasn't, then he was a liar. If Jesus really believed he was God but actually wasn't, then he was insane, a lunatic.

People do not follow liars or lunatics for long. If a leader is a liar, they are eventually found out. Jesus performed a lot of miracles that could have been debunked by people at the time. When the Roman government started persecuting and killing Christians, the early disciples would have just given up the lie rather than suffer and die for it. When persecution came, the lie would have broken down.

But maybe Jesus was just a really charismatic lunatic who simply believed he was God. If he were simply crazy but compelling, he might have gained some followers—after all, dynamic crazy people gain followers all the time. But, once these same crazies are arrested or die, their followers end up following someone else.

We can see both of these scenarios played out through history. Yet Jesus remains. Logically, then, Jesus was—and is—who he said he was—the Messiah, the Lord, the divine Son of God. And that is important.

OWNING UP

We all get things wrong—a lot. I know that I do, for sure. I am not always a good friend, husband, father, or co-worker. There have been many times in my life that I have needed to ask forgiveness from others. I do things that can hurt relationships, and I need to make those things right.

In my history of frequently being in the wrong, I have learned that there are a couple of things I need to do to be reconciled with someone:

> *I need to feel sorry for the wrong I have done.*
> *I need to apologize.*
> *I need to be forgiven.*
> *I need to make up for the wrong I have done.*

Any of these steps can happen without the others, but without all of them in the proper order I do not end up reconciled. There are times I have done something wrong but haven't felt sorry. There are times I have apologized but have not been forgiven. Sometimes people have forgiven me even though I had not yet apologized. So these steps happen individually all the time, but when they don't all happen a rift still exists in a relationship.

The wrongs we commit also impact our relationship with God. Certain wrongs, those that break the moral law given us by God, we call *sin*—and we can sin against God and each other. The reality is that our sins have an impact on us in this life and in the next. Every sin damages our relationship with God— even if it only seems to involve another person. Much like secondhand smoke, our sin always affects another, whether or not we realize it or want to admit it. Jesus speaks about this truth when he tells his disciples that when they refuse to help the homeless, hungry, and sick, they are actually hurting him (see Matthew 25:31–46).

Sin breaks our relationship with God. Reconciliation with God, though, looks a little different than reconciliation with others. God is God, so we are not on an even playing field. God is not a peer; he is our creator. When we sin against God, we are hurting our relationship with the very being who is the source of our existence and holds dominion over us. This can make it tough to really be reconciled with God.

We can say we are sorry for our sin. We can even feel sorry for our sins. But we cannot really make up—in theological terms, *atone*—for our sins.

Throughout history, people tried through sacrifices to atone for their sins, but these were not sufficient. Regardless of how many sacrifices they offered, they would not be able to ever really make atonement for what they had done. They would sin against God again and again and repeatedly seek his mercy and forgiveness. Beyond that, they had no real way of knowing if God had actually forgiven them. How would they know if their sacrifices were enough? How would they know if God was going to leave their sins in the past or if he was still angry?

This is why Jesus is so important. Jesus came, as the Son of God, to make the perfect sacrifice of atonement on the Cross and reconcile us definitively with God.

St. Paul was an early follower of Jesus and is responsible for writing a good portion of the New Testament, i.e., his letters to the various Christian communities of the first century. He bluntly summarizes the problem with sin—namely, everyone commits it (see Romans 3:23) and the punishment for sin is death (see Romans 6:23). That means, because our sins offend an eternal God by violating the moral order established by him, being in a state of sinfulness deserves the maximum punishment, which is death. Because God is eternal, the ultimate punishment of rejecting a relationship with him through unrepentant sin must be eternal.

THE BAD NEWS

There are many images of what this eternal punishment—commonly known as *hell*—might look like, but one thing is certain: Hell is the eternal separation of our souls from God, and God is love (see 1 John 4:8). That means that hell is a separation from Love itself for all of eternity. This is what hell feels like. It is actually unfathomable: a love-less existence. It feels like never feeling or knowing love or loving another—forever.

God does not want anyone to end up in hell, which is why he sent Jesus. At the end of the day, though, he has given us freedom—the freedom to love him or reject him. God cannot force us to love him; love, by definition, must be given freely. There is no such thing as forced love. This is why sin separates us from God, who, as we have seen, is Love. So God honors our free will—either we choose to love him or not by our actions. Unfortunately, if we make the wrong choice and sin, we can end up eternally separated from God.

In the end, though, nothing we can do can ever makes full atonement for the debt we owe due to our sins. Every sin has a cost, and we cannot pay ours. We cannot ever be really reconciled with God on our own.

God, being perfect justice, cannot go against his own nature and simply dismiss our sins. When we sin, we break our covenant with him, and this carries with it the natural consequence of separation from him. God is also perfect Love (see 1 John 4:8), so he does not dismiss us, either. Rather, he designed a way to atone for sin in an act of perfect love. God chose to reconcile us to himself by completing the last two steps. This is why Jesus is so important.

THE GOOD NEWS

Jesus is fully God and fully human; he has a body. This means that Jesus, while on the earth, felt what you and I feel, and experienced life the way we do. In fact, it is accepted Christian teaching that Jesus was like us in all things except sin. He had favorite foods just like we do, laughed with friends, and felt the full spectrum of human emotions, including sadness, joy, and anger (though without sin). Jesus understood headaches and sunburns, hunger and sleepless nights. He understands the totality of our human experience.

Through the witness of his life, Jesus shows us how to live in freedom, how to love God and our neighbor. He then dies on a cross to set us free from the punishment we deserve for our sins. He takes our sins on himself and makes atonement for them. Every time we look at a cross, we need to remember

Heaven came
to earth
to bring
earth back
to heaven.

that we have been forgiven by the death and resurrection of Jesus, not by our own decision or accord (see Romans 5:8).

In his bodily resurrection from the dead, Jesus makes eternal life possible for us because his death forgives our sins and atones for the eternal separation those sins cause. If Jesus were not God as well as human, this would not be possible; he would just be another random person dying by crucifixion. He could have been a really good person, even the best person who ever lived, but he would not have been able to save us.

This was the essential message of Jesus. His entire life was preparing his followers for his death so that they would come to understand how to really live. During his public ministry, Jesus laid the groundwork for the Church by giving authority to his apostles to celebrate the Eucharist and the other sacraments. It is through the sacraments that we experience God's grace in tangible ways. They are the means God uses to make us holy.

In short, Jesus uses the Church to help save us. His very name in Aramaic, *Yeshua*, literally means "God saves." Heaven came to earth to bring earth back to heaven. We call that the Gospel, the "good news."

SAVING OURSELVES ... AND OTHER FANTASIES

We cannot save ourselves. We really want to, though. But we do not need to!

When I was growing up, I saw myself as a lone wolf, as the only person I could trust. In grade school, I didn't have many friends and was usually the first person picked on. In junior high, I discovered that I couldn't trust my friends, who were often fickle and quick to leave me hanging when trouble surfaced. In high school, I realized that if I wanted to do something, I should do it myself—and in college, I believed that I was the master of my own destiny.

So, you could say that I made myself my own savior.

This can easily happen to anyone. Others let us down and hurt us. We see how well things seemingly go when we hold the steering wheel of our lives. We determine that, even if we failed, at least we know that we were the cause of our failure, not someone else.

We drill this mentality into people in an effort to empower them. We challenge young people to take ownership of their lives and to make their own decisions. This is good, but it can spiral into an erroneous attitude that we are ultimately in control of our lives and are responsible for our own salvation. When we hit a difficult time, this illusion quickly unravels and leaves us in pieces.

We cannot save ourselves from our sins. If we try to face the brokenness and hurt of our lives alone, we will eventually fall into despair. Jesus offers us forgiveness, mercy, and salvation— and also a companion to walk with during the course of our lives.

Remember, Jesus was like us in all things but sin. Jesus experienced being abandoned, heartbroken, anxious, sad, angry, and joyful. So we have a God who knows who we are and our condition because he himself experienced it. Jesus extends forgiveness and healing to each of us but does not force us to accept it. We need to choose to accept his invitation.

What are you looking for? What do you desire? Has it given you hope? Has it offered you something more than an endless cycle of always wanting something new or something more? Does it bring you comfort in times of sorrow?

If it isn't Jesus, then it can't.

Only Jesus can save you.

Maybe you have been going through the motions in your faith, but have never really plugged into it. Maybe you have known about Jesus your whole life, but you don't really know Jesus. Maybe you have always considered yourself as part of the ninety-nine, but are now realizing that you are really the "one" who is lost. I realize this more and more every day. Conversion is not a one-time thing; it is a daily calling.

Jesus *wants* to save you.

We can think of salvation from a collective perspective, i.e., Jesus came to save the world, but not me, personally. Perhaps you have seen the famous verse on banners at stadiums, John 3:16—"For God so loved the world that he gave his only begotten Son, that whoever believes in him should not perish but have eternal life." We can be spiritually short sighted and focus only on the world part. Jesus died for you! He wants to save you … unique, irreplaceable, unrepeatable you. Jesus leaves ninety-nine to go after the one. That one is you. That one is me. Jesus wants you to be reconciled to God, but the choice is yours, and it is a choice of faith.

You and I need to have faith that God exists and wants a relationship with us, and there is a good reason for this faith. We need to believe that Jesus was who he said he was—the

Messiah, the divine Son of God—and that Jesus, through his life, death, and resurrection, saves us from our sins.

This requires a (slight) leap of faith. We need not only to accept who Jesus is, but also we are called to embrace the Church he founded, the community of faith he established to teach and minister in his name. We cannot make this leap on our own; we need God's help.

Now, put this book down and simply sit in silence for a moment. Become aware that God is present with you, right now. Ask him for the gift of faith. Invite God into your life in a new way. If you have never spoken the words, "Jesus, I need you and accept you as my savior. I can't save myself. I need you" or something similar, speak them now. You do not need to have it all figured out. You do not need to have all the answers. You do not need to be sinless. Even if you have considered yourself a follower of Jesus for years, recommit to him now.

You can begin following Jesus in a new way, right now.

A REAL RELATIONSHIP WITH JESUS

Every January, countless people start working out but stop after only a few sessions (or never came back after an initial consultation). They made a decision to change their lifestyle, but they are not really committed. When things become difficult or they actually need to make substantial changes to their diet and routine, they simply quit and go back to their old way of life.

I hope that in the last few minutes you have made a new commitment to Jesus. I hope that you have made a decision to stop trying to be your own savior and to embrace Christ.

The journey is just beginning.

Jesus promised disciples abundant life (see John 10:10). Some in our modern age claim that believing in God or being religious diminishes one's quality of life. The exact opposite is true. When we follow Jesus, we experience the fullness of what life has to offer. Remember, God is love. To experience a relationship with God is to begin to explore the very depths of love itself and embark on an adventure with the One who created and loves you. How could this be anything but exciting?

This decision requires what any relationship requires—commitment. We show our commitment to our friendships and romantic relationships through quality time, loyalty, a willingness to grow in knowledge, and a desire to avoid anything that would hurt the relationship.

Our relationship with Jesus must be no different.

First, we spend quality time worshiping Jesus. This does not mean that we retreat from the world, but simply that we are mindful in our faith and our relationship with Jesus comes first. It is the foundation of our lives, and it shapes our decisions throughout the day. We begin to ask, "Am I putting Jesus first in my life, or is something else motivating me?" No one is perfect in their walk with Jesus. We all get distracted by other pursuits, but if we remain mindful of when we take our eyes of Christ and become fixated on something else, we can catch ourselves and regain focus.

When we enter into a relationship with Jesus, we need to spend time with him in prayer if it is going to grow. We know how we drift away from our friends when we stop communicating. In a similar way, though Jesus is never far from us, our hearts can become far from him when we stop seeking him in prayer.

> Prayer *is* your relationship with God.

The Church offers us many ways to pray, both individually and communally. The communal prayer of the Mass is the most important communal prayer we have been given. We gather as a faith community, receive the Eucharist, and are strengthened together in prayer. We can gather in smaller groups to pray various devotional prayers (e.g., the Rosary, novenas, and the Divine Mercy chaplet) as a community, as well. Structured prayer is great for developing the good habit and rhythm of praying, but prayer can also be free-flowing, organic, and spontaneous. Just talk to God!

Don't worry if your initial conversations with God seem one-sided, as if you are talking to yourself. Simply ask him to walk with you and help you become quiet so you can hear his voice. Ask him to reveal any specific areas that he wants you to reflect on and thank him for the good things with which he has blessed you. Ask for his help with specific issues in your life. Your spontaneous prayers do not need to be long or well-structured. Simply pour out your heart, honestly, to your loving Creator.

Prayer is the very lifeblood of our relationship with Jesus. It is where we spend our quality time with the Lord. Make no mistake, prayer does not merely help your relationship with God—prayer is your relationship with God. If you do not have time set aside currently to pray, make the time, put it into your calendar. Find friends to commit to praying with you. Make attending Mass a priority every Sunday. In the midst of busy schedules, we make time for what we care about, so make Jesus the first person you make time for every week.

GROWING IN RELATIONSHIP WITH JESUS

As a relationship between two people deepens, they grow in knowledge of each other. When we love someone, we desire to learn more about them and as we learn more about those we love, we often love them even more. There is a lot to learn about Jesus and our Catholic Faith. Be willing to learn and grow. Find some good books to grow in your knowledge of the Faith. Ask questions from people you trust and you know are knowledgeable. Never stop learning about Jesus.

Finally, in our walk with the Lord, we have to leave some things behind. If we love someone, we avoid doing things that hurt that person and negatively impact our relationship with that person. As we have seen, sin harms our relationship with God. Following Jesus means making a commitment to avoid sin. Of course, we may slip back into old habits of sin, but part of our commitment is seeking reconciliation when we do and return to walking with Jesus. That can mean some tough decisions, especially if there are areas of our lives that we know are hurting us, others, and God. Being a new person sometimes means other parts of our lives need to die so they can also be made new in Christ.

All of this is worth it. Nothing can compare to the abundant life that Jesus offers us every day we walk with him. Jesus is more than a story, myth, or historical figure. He is God, Savior, and he is seeking you and calling you to follow him. So what exactly does this daily relationship with Jesus really look like? What does it require? Before you turn the page, pray, "Come, Holy Spirit" several times silently. To live this life, you are going to need the Spirit's guidance and power.

Discussion Questions ⎯⎯⎯⎯⎯⎯⎯

1. In your view, what is the most compelling evidence that Jesus is who he claimed to be—the divine Son of God?

2. Do you believe sin damages your relationship with God?

3. Do you accept that unrepented sin can keep one from eternal life in heaven? Why or why not?

4. Based on your previous answer, how do you view the necessity of Jesus in your life?

5. Which of the following titles of Jesus resonates most with you? Teacher, Healer, Helper, or Savior.

6. What role does prayer have in your daily life? What keeps you from praying more?

A Life with Jesus

N ow what?

Let's take a step back and review what we have learned:

God is real.

Jesus is the divine Son of God, the Messiah, who came to save us.

Jesus wants a personal relationship with me.

What comes next? Why is attending church so important, since Mass is often uninspired and unengaging?

These were the questions I asked throughout my teens and twenties. I was in a constant state of conversion, teetering between living for myself and trying to give it all to God.

I had always thought of conversion as a one-time thing, as more of a transaction than a relationship with God. I wanted to be part of God's club and be saved from hell, but I didn't really want all the extra stuff that came with living my life for him. My attitude was, "I'll take heaven, Lord, but you can keep chastity and obedience. Give me peace of mind and financial freedom, but hold the self-sacrifice and suffering." Truth be told, many Christians feel the same way. It's only natural.

I mean, who really wants suffering? Who really wants to give up his or her own will and follow God's? Who really wants to put others before self?

I wanted the water of baptism—that is, to be part of God's family—but not the death that comes with it: death to sin, to selfishness, and to the world. At its core, baptism is about dying to sin so that we are free to live a new life with Christ. As

St. Paul writes, "Do you not know that all of us who have been baptized into Christ Jesus were baptized into his death? We were buried therefore with him by baptism into death, so that as Christ was raised from the dead by the glory of the Father, we too might walk in newness of life" (Romans 6:3-5).

Similarly, I desired the blood of Jesus—that is, the blood that he shed to free me from my sins and selfishness and pride— but not the suffering that comes with the blood. I wanted the reward of Easter Sunday without first enduring the pains of Good Friday.

It is telling, though, that when the Roman soldier pierced the side of Jesus on the Cross that both blood and water flowed out of the wound. We are reminded of the need for the transformative power of blood and water—upon the altar at every Mass, when wine is transformed into the blood of Christ co-mingled with water. This serves as a perpetual reminder that the sacraments flow from Jesus' sacrifice—and that our deepest connection to Jesus is through communion with his Church.

Some take issue with the Church and its practices, accusing it of being out-of-touch with the times and its rituals archaic. But it is in the Church's traditions and teachings that we discover our identity, our true north. It is precisely through these practices—especially the sacraments—that we enter into a true relationship with God and others.

THE LIGHT (BULB) OF THE WORLD?

There's an old joke that goes something like this: "How many Catholics does it take to change a light bulb"? The punch line: "None. Catholics don't like to *change* anything."

The implication is that the Church, throughout its history, has always been slow to change.

With that in mind, a few years back I came up with a variation of the punchline:

"None. We use candles."

Well, I thought it was funny, anyway.

Whenever we enter a Catholic church, every candle, every stained glass window, every holy water font, every crucifix reminds us that we are joined to something far greater than ourselves. We hear the same readings each week as our fellow Catholics around the world. We pray the same prayers. We assume the same postures. We enter into the same sacrifice— the unique, transcendent, eternal sacrifice of Jesus on the Cross—being re-presented on thousands of altars throughout the world.

Every minute of every day, somewhere in the world, Mass is being celebrated, and the timeless sacrifice of Jesus is being experienced by his followers. In the Mass, we encounter our past (Christ's sacrificial death on the Cross for our sins), experience our present (the community of faith celebrating our salvation in Christ), and get a foretaste of our future (eternal life with God in heaven). Even for practicing Catholics, these are big realities to wrap our heads around. The Mass, though happening all the time, is actually timeless. The past, present and future meet within it.

So, yes, we use candles, holy water, crosses, and vestments— for good reason.

The point here is that while the Church does not change its teachings, this is not because it is arbitrarily stubborn or rigid but because it is humble. The apostles received what was handed on to them by Christ and, following his command, handed it on to others (see Matthew 28:19; 1 Corinthians 11; Acts 2). Over the centuries, their successors, the bishops, have continued to pass on the truths of the Faith. Even with all the scandal and heartbreak fostered by the Church's leaders—which God warned us about in the Scriptures (see Jeremiah 23, John 11)—we must remember that the Church, like Christ, is both human and divine. The Church is still animated, protected, and led by the Holy Spirit, even when its very human leaders sin. The failure of its members does not empty the Church of its divine foundation or invalidate the truth of its teachings.

Perspective is everything when it comes to the faith.

FROM "YOU SHALL NOT" TO "YOU SHALL"

Most people tend to see the Ten Commandments as an oppressive list of rules that prescribe what they cannot do. I certainly did. After all, eight of the commandments begin with "you shall not"! But this is from the perspective of man, not of the Spirit—a perspective God repeatedly warns us against in the Bible.

Let's see how context and perspective—how living in Christ—can shape our understanding of the Commandments.

On the left, we have a literal paraphrase of the Commandments, the "shall nots." On the right, we see how these divine commands lead a humble soul pursuing spiritual freedom into fulfillment in Christ.

The Law (Commandments)	Life in Christ (Fulfillment)
You shall not ...	You shall ...
... have other gods before me.	... be single-hearted toward me.
... take the Lord's name in vain.	... be reverent in speech and conduct.
... dishonor the Sabbath.	... keep your priorities centered on God.
... kill.	... protect and defend life.
... commit adultery.	... be faithful to vocation and human dignity.
... steal.	... be trustworthy.
... bear false witness.	... be honest in word and deed.
... covet thy neighbor's wife.	... have only pure intentions and desires.
... covet thy neighbor's goods.	... be grateful for what you possess.

Did you see the subtle difference that an intentional life in Christ makes? Both versions of the Commandments accomplish the same thing, but the Holy Spirit gives us the ability to go deeper.

Many Christians do not really understand the role of the Holy Spirit in their lives. This goes for cradle Catholics as well.

Let us briefly consider why.

As Christians, we have received the revelation that God is a Trinity—three divine Persons who share a single divine nature. As Jesus said, "I and the Father are one" (John 10:30) and "Make disciples of all nations, baptizing them in the name of the Father and of the Son and of the Holy Spirit" (Matthew 28:19-20). God's nature, of course, is the most profound mystery we can ponder; after all, God is infinite and we are finite. We can come up with images to make the mystery of the Trinity a little more manageable.

We think of God the Father as an elderly man with a white beard, flowing robes, and sandals, enthroned in heaven. He sits in judgment of all mankind, condemning the wicked and smiting them—but hopefully not us.

We see Jesus as more approachable than the Father. After all, he is human as well as divine. He came to us as an infant in a manger, then became a friend (as well as a teacher) to his followers, and finally suffered and died for us on the Cross. If we look deeper, we can see him in one another, within the priesthood and the sacraments, especially in the Holy Eucharist.

We are not quite sure what to do with the Holy Spirit, however. The biblical images of fire, wind, and dove are helpful, but can also cause anxiety for most of us control freaks. After all, we cannot control fire or the wind (or a dove, for that matter!). It is as though, since we cannot control the dove, we would rather put it in a cage than let it fly free in our lives.

Again, this is where most Catholics (and, truthfully, nearly all people) today get it wrong about God. Many believe that it is God's job to make us happy. Actually, it is not. The job of the Holy Spirit is not to make us happy, but to make us *holy*. The

Holy Spirit wants us to move outside of our comfort zones. The gifts the Spirit unleashes threaten to make us uneasy and may even seem quite odd not only to others but also to ourselves. No, when it comes to this divine Third Person of the Trinity most of us are more comfortable extinguishing the flame and caging the bird. It is less messy that way.

HAPPINESS OR JOY?

We can fall into the trap of thinking that God desires our happiness. Actually, he desires something far greater for us—joy. As Jesus taught his disciples, "These things [the Gospel] I have spoken to you, that *my joy may be in you, and that your joy may be full*" (John15:11, emphasis added). St. Paul affirms that one of the fruits of a life lived in the Holy Spirit is joy (see Galatians 5:22). While Disneyland promises happiness, God offers us irretrievable and incomparable joy—forever.

How do we experience this joy in the Spirit? By striving to be holy. And how do we live holy lives? By living in accord with the teachings of Jesus.

As Jesus promised his apostles, "When the Spirit of truth comes, he will guide you into all the truth" (John 16:13). St. Paul echoes these word of Jesus when he encourages the Christians in Ephesus to "put on the new man, created after the likeness of God in true righteousness and holiness" (Ephesians 4:24). And, as St. Peter writes, "As he who called you is holy, be holy yourselves in all your conduct, since it is written, 'You shall be holy, for I am holy'" (1 Peter 1:16).

So, is there a tension between holiness and happiness or, more to the point, holiness and joy? After all, if holiness means following the teachings of Christ rather than my own desires, doesn't that mean that I will be less joyful? The two seem opposed ... but are they really?

KEEP THE CHANGE?

In my late teens, the lights finally started to come on spiritually, and I began to realize that the spiritual life—that is, living a truly Catholic life in relationship with God—was not at all what I thought it would be.

"You've changed." I heard these words more than once from my friends.

Is there a greater dig you can take at someone who has begun to take the faith seriously? On the other hand, is there a more affirming observation? These words can bring about either an intense, defensive rebuttal or a humbled, sincere gratitude—or a mixture of both.

At seventeen, I took them as a proclamation of war. Not long before, I had experienced my first moment of conversion while on a youth retreat, and I had decided to follow Jesus—or at least try to. There was no turning back.

While this decision was great for my soul, it wreaked havoc on my social life. I went from being a popular high school junior to living an almost leper-like existence of being ostracized and excluded in my senior year. I was trying to live in the light—a light that many of my friends had found to be a bit too blinding.

When a buddy of mine told me that I had changed, this felt more hurtful than any insult he could have directed my way.

"No, I haven't!" I shouted, with insecure indignation.

"Yes, you have," he said. "You're totally different. You went on that retreat and nothing has been the same."

He was right, of course. He had proclaimed a truth I wasn't ready to hear. On the retreat, I had come face to face with God's love and mercy, and everything had changed. All of a sudden I

> Jesus doesn't want you to lose the good things in your life; he wants to amplify them.

knew that God was real and that he was pursuing me, along with everyone else. At that moment, I realized that I was that "one" lost sheep that the Good Shepherd had left the ninety-nine to go and rescue. I ran away, but the Shepherd chased after me and brought me into his flock.

Sheep may be lost, but the Shepherd always seeks to find them.

I couldn't deny it. I couldn't fight it. I just had to embrace it. In that moment, I realized my friend was being more honest than I was. I had changed, praised be to God! It was time to stop running away from God and walk with him. I still had to learn what this meant, though—to come to understand what St. Paul wrote about to the Galatians:

> I have been crucified with Christ; *it is no longer I who live, but Christ who lives in me;* and the life I now live in the flesh I live by faith in the Son of God,
>
> who loved me and gave himself for me. (Galatians 2:20, emphasis added)

When we start to see that the Christian faith is not about our search for God but, rather, his searching and longing for us everything changes. When we see in the Faith the intimacy that God offers us through the Church and its sacraments, we begin to see everything from a new perspective.

In Christ, we allow the Holy Spirit to form our minds and hearts. With the Spirit, we take off the rose-colored glasses and see things as they truly are. When our lives are led by the Spirit—the same Holy Spirit who inspired the Scriptures and who continues to inspire and guide the Church—we finally see 20/20.

It is in Christ that the Bible—which can be confusing and seem outdated—is read in its proper context.

It is in Christ that the Ten Commandments go from being a negative to a positive, offering a life of truth, beauty, and virtue rather than a morbid list of "you shall nots."

It is in Christ that this Church, while very human and filled with sinners, is also divine and full of saints.

SAINTS ALIVE!

Jesus presented his disciples with some pretty hard-hitting paradoxes: If you want to be the greatest, then be the least (see Mark 9:35; Matthew 23:11) if you want to live, then you must die (see Matthew 16:25; Mark 8:35; Luke 9:24). This is only possible in Christ, through the power of the Spirit.

In the Gospels, we are reminded that only after losing what we consider living do we find true life (see Matthew 10:39). When we find something that we realize is the greatest thing in the world, everything else is worth losing (see Luke 15). Jesus promises his followers abundant life—a life beyond what they could achieve on their own (see John 10:10).

Yet, many get stuck on what they need to lose (see Mark 10:17-31) to gain the life that Jesus promises. Jesus does not want you to lose the good things in your life; he wants to amplify them. What about the bad things, the attitudes and behaviors that are harmful and holding you back from really living? These are the areas that Jesus wants to bring healing and renewal.

We see what living a true, abundant life looks like when we read about the saints. The fisherman Simon (later St. Peter) and his brother Andrew were mending their nets when Jesus called them to be apostles. On that particular day, Simon's and Andrew's lives changed. Working through the night, they had not caught any fish—which was a bit of a problem for professional fishermen, particularly from an income standpoint. In their encounter, Jesus asks them to try again. Understandably, they are a bit incredulous; here is this stranger, a rabbi no less, telling them, fisherman by trade, how to do their job. But Peter and Andrew give it another shot. The result, of course, is an abundant catch. Jesus asks them to leave it behind and follow him, and they immediately leave their boat and nets behind.

There was probably a lot going on in Peter's and Andrew's hearts at that moment, and perhaps even some tension at walking away from the only life that they knew, but they choose to walk away from the catch of fish (and the money it would have brought in) and follow Jesus. The Lord did not magically change them into something that they were not; he took who they were and elevated it. Peter and Andrew were not going to be catching fish anymore; they were going to be catching men and women for Jesus.

What would you give up to become the person you were meant to be? What would you let go of to become fully alive? To stop merely breathing and begin truly living? That is worth more than any amount of money or worldly success. Peter and Andrew faced such a choice, and they chose well.

The same is true for St. Francis of Assisi (1181–1226) and St. Ignatius of Loyola (1491–1556). Both men dreamed of being knights and gaining victory in battle. Francis came from a wealthy family and, while he aspired to become a knight, he never actually saw serious battle. On the other hand, before his conversion, Ignatius actually was a soldier for a Spanish nobleman. It was only after his leg was shattered in battle by a cannon ball that he began to seek another life.

Both Francis and Ignatius ended up fighting a different kind of battle. Each was called by God to engage in a spiritual fight during their specific time, and each founded a religious order to serve this battle, and both the Franciscans and Jesuits still exist to this day. Their spiritual disciplines have inspired millions of people to discern right from wrong, resist evil, and love God and their neighbors. They became spiritual heroes, both of their time and throughout the ages. Both found profound, lasting joy in following Jesus and were zealous in leading others to know him.

This zeal for Christ and joy in life is a trait that can been seen in every saint. While every saint's story has a different starting point, they all share a common destination in Christ. St. Thérèse of Lisieux (1873–1897), for example, lived a short life marked by illness and frailty—but with a deep, intimate, and joyful love of Jesus. She did not do anything remarkable; she entered religious life at fifteen and spent the rest of her life as a cloistered Carmelite nun. But Thérèse lived with great joy and impressed the love of Christ upon everyone she encountered, until she passed away at twenty-four. At the request of her superior, Thérèse wrote a memoir of her life, *Story of a Soul*, which presented her "little way" of following in simple acts of love. This approach resonated with many who were seeking a way to follow Jesus in everyday life. Thérèse's insights were so profound in their simplicity—and her witness so compelling— that she was named a Doctor of the Church, an honorary title bestowed on those saints who have made significant contributions to theology or doctrine through their writings.

Saintly stories such as these are countless. The saints show us that we do not become less ourselves in Christ, we become more. We do not actually lose something, we gain Someone—and this Someone does not just promise us abundant life on earth, but eternal life in heaven.

HOW ABOUT YOU?

Now, you might be thinking, Me, a saint? No way! Sainthood isn't for me. It is for holy people like Father No-Nonsense or Sister Mary Strict ... or my grandmother ... but not me! I'm shooting for good 'ole purgatory. Just tell me what I need to do to avoid hell.

This was my philosophy for the better part of my youth. I was convinced that if I abandoned my own goals and best-laid plans and placed myself at the feet of Jesus that I would be destined to journey through life never laughing or smiling or enjoying anything again. I was certain that a life of holiness—of seeking to be a saint—would mean paralyzing boredom and predictability.

Then, I learned an invaluable lesson. It was as though the Holy Spirit took me on a walk—almost like the (holy) Ghost of Christmas Present in Dickens' *A Christmas Carol*—and showed me all the holiest people I had ever met in my life. All different ages and backgrounds, stories and struggles, with differing vocations and walks of life, and, aside from prayer and passion, the two things they all had in common were unshakeable joy and a sense of humor.

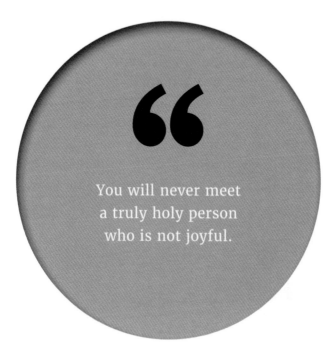

You will never meet
a truly holy person
who is not joyful.

It's true. After a completely unscientific study, it seems clear that you will never meet a truly holy person who is not joyful and laughs easily. Sure, you will meet devout and pious souls along the way, but truly holy souls know how to laugh.

As Dostoyevsky wrote in *The Brothers Karamazov*, "If you love ... you will perceive *the divine mystery* in things. Once you perceive it, you will begin to comprehend it better every day. And you will come at last to love the whole world with an all-embracing love."[3]

Perhaps Jesus and St. Paul were right. Maybe a life led by the Holy Spirit really will lead us to truth and beauty, to goodness, joy, and peace. When we encounter true love, all we want is to remain in it. And when we encounter God's love—so different from conditional human love —our perspective changes. Our days are no longer something to survive but opportunities to thrive, by living out a mission, a purpose, an adventure, much like the saints.

BUCKLE UP

If you had the choice between riding a carousel or a roller coaster, which would you choose?

A carousel is safe and predictable. It turns, but it doesn't really go anywhere. Riding it can become somewhat monotonous after a few spins.

A roller coaster, on the other hand, offers a surge of adrenaline. When the lap bar comes down and latches, you know that something a bit more exciting—and dangerous, relatively speaking—than a spin on a carousel is about to happen. Sure,

---

[3]   Fyodor Dostoevsky, *The Brothers Karamazov* – Illustrated Platinum Edition, page 273

you are securely strapped in, but the track seems awfully steep and fast, and those turns up ahead.

The spiritual life is more like a roller coaster than a carousel.

Many of us roll through life claiming to follow God, but what we really want is control over our lives. We don't want to surrender our feeling of control, of safety, and trust that God is guiding us along the sometimes bumpy and scary tracks of life. So, we opt for the spiritual carousel. We want the ride of life to be smooth and comfortable, without too many jolts and bumps and hills and turns. We want to know exactly how it is going to turn out and feel like we are in complete control.

The saints did not opt for the carousel.

A life led by the Holy Spirit is a life of trust and surrender. It says, "I'm in the car, Lord, but you're driving. Take me where you want me to go."

True surrender to the Spirit, though, is not easy. This can only come about with a steady and consistent ongoing prayer life, along with community and accountability. There is a reason Jesus sent out his disciples two by two. Living the Christian life requires a shared faith; one does not live it as an individual. Seek out like-minded (and like-hearted), faith-filled people who will hold you accountable. These could be your family, friends, neighbors, or parishioners, those souls who care enough about you and your spiritual life to ride the roller coaster with you. If no one immediately comes to mind, begin praying now for the Lord to send someone like that into your life.

You might start and then stumble. You might fall repeatedly, but Jesus is there with his nail-scarred hands wide open, ready and willing to pick you up again and again. His mercy is divine, and it is limitless. Jesus is always ready to give you the grace you need through the Church and its sacraments. Just keep going to him. Keep moving forward.

Remember that you are not alone in your journey of faith. Many others are also on the path to joy, as they seek a deeper relationship with Christ. You are going to become more, not less. Your life is about to become more abundant, not diminished. Life only gets better from here and what comes next is better than anything you could ever imagine.

This is where life really gets interesting.

Discussion Questions

1. Do you believe that God is in control of your life or are you? Do you find letting God be in control a struggle or a joy? Why do you think this might be?

2. Explain what having a relationship with the Holy Spirit means to you. How do you—or could you—invite God into your daily decisions?

3. Do you ever reflect on the Ten Commandments? How often do you think of their role in shaping your life?

4. On a scale of one to ten, how open are you to change? (One being "very closed" to change, ten being "totally open.")

5. Are you inspired the lives of the saints? Do you see them as un-reachable examples of virtue?

Jesus Loves Me ... So Now What?

D uring my freshman year of college, a priest posed a riddle to me that changed the course of my life. I was seventeen, two thousand miles from home, and quite taken with my newfound college boy freedom. I am sure he knew that I was long on ambition but short on direction.

Over a basket of buffalo wings after Mass one Sunday, Father looked intently at me and asked, "Mark, do you want to know the secret of life?"

A bit sarcastically, I replied, "Sure, Father, I would *love* to know the secret of life ... but hey, could we get another basket of wings?"

Wow, I thought, *so this guy has the answer to life's greatest mystery ... yeah, right!*

I am embarrassed by how little I knew back then.

"Lean in," he said, over the din of the restaurant.

Intrigued, I leaned forward, awaiting some proverbial wisdom, a golden nugget for the ages. Would it be a quote from Scripture? An aphorism of Plato? Perhaps a gem from St. Thomas Aquinas? Or perhaps Tony Robbins?

"Fish swim, birds fly," he said, with a wry grin.

Afraid to look ignorant, I quickly covered up the look of confusion on my face and replied with a sustained, "Hmmm."

He then repeated, "Fish swim, birds fly, Mark."

With that, he got up and left ... leaving me with the bill, a now empty wallet, and a million questions. (Father, if you are reading this, you still owe me fifteen dollars!).

A few days later, I ran into this man of God coming out of class. I asked him to explain his cryptic secret to life and he merely repeated himself, "Fish swim, birds fly."

Finally, the following Sunday, I waited outside the sanctuary after Mass.

"Father," I said, jokingly, "If you don't explain your secret to life to me, you might need to call a brother priest to come anoint you."

"It's simple, Mark," he replied. "Fish swim and birds fly ... we give glory to God by doing what we are designed to do. As far as I can see, you aren't doing it."

> We give glory to God by doing what we are designed to do.

I really pondered these words, and in the months that followed, I began to look at my life with a newfound sense of purpose and wonder—as a mystery not to be solved but to behold. I came to realize that if I was going to fulfill my true purpose— my God-given vocation—and put all of the gifts, talents, and blessings I had been given, I would need to get to know God intimately. My story was just beginning. As the lead character of that story, I had to get to know its Author firsthand.

PRACTICALLY SPEAKING

In this book, we have covered a lot of ground on our journey. Now we have come to the proverbial fork in the road. Which path are you going to take? Is the reality of God's existence and love for you drawing your heart to move further, to go deeper, or blaze a new path?

Will you head further down the road toward accepting God's invitation to intimacy?

Through the beauty of Christ and his Church, you can grow in intimacy with God and begin to more readily and easily hear him and see his presence in your life.

Here are a few tangible ways to immediately experience the love and mercy of Christ.

THINK *INSIDE* THE BOX

If you are Catholic, the best place to press reset on your spiritual life and immediately give it a big boost is through the sacrament of Reconciliation (or confession). In that little confessional box, freedom and peace await you.

If you haven't been to confession in a while, don't walk there— *run*.

Take time to prepare. Examine your conscience. Go online and read through an examination or look for one at your parish church to help you take account of where you have fallen.

Hide nothing. Justify nothing. Avoid word games. Just sit with Jesus, in the person of the priest, and relay *own* your sins. Acknowledge your weakness and your need for Jesus, your Savior.

Take your penance seriously. This can be easily overlooked, but it is an essential part of the sacrament of reconciliation. As Bishop Fulton Sheen explains:

> Suppose that I told one of these little children that every time they did anything wrong they were to put a nail into a (wooden) board. Can you imagine that? Every time you did wrong, disobeyed your mother, for example, you were to drive a nail into the board. Then every time your mother forgave you, and you said you were sorry, the mother would tell you to pull the nail out.
>
> Is there anything left? What is left? A hole is left. That is the effect of sin.

Even though the sin is forgiven, we have to make some reparation for it and that is the reason you are given a penance in confession, to fill up the holes. And to help us make adequate reparation for sin, we have the intercession of the saints and the mercy of our Blessed Lord.

When we go to confession, our lives are completely changed by submitting to the Mercy of God."[4]

God's grace is real and efficacious. Go avail yourself of Jesus' mercy. It is impossible for us to hear the voice of the Lord if our souls are dying in sin. The three most freeing words are not "I love you" but, rather, "I absolve you."

Repent. Reconcile. Restart.

RECLAIM YOUR SABBATH

Do you consider Sunday the end of your week or the beginning? Because of Christ's resurrection from the dead on that glorious first Easter Sunday morning, thousands of Jewish Christians who had previously worshiped the Lord on the seventh day, Saturday, began to do so on Sunday. With Sunday Eucharist established as the new Sabbath, the focus of the week for followers of Christ also shifted.

As the first day of the week, Sunday prepares us for all that lies ahead for the next six days. Today, among many Catholics, the commandment to "Remember the sabbath day, to keep it holy" (Exodus 20:8) has been reduced to spending an hour in church at Sunday Mass, if that. But this is the bare minimum in maintaining our relationship with God. What we need to do is fill every Sunday with rest, prayer, and spending time with our family and faith community. Imagine if you shifted your necessary tasks—things such as shopping, laundry, yard work,

[4]   See https://www.youtube.com/watch?v=wNZPvk6wB6k

or paying bills—to other days of the week, leaving Sunday free to enter into communion with God and loved ones. Enjoy the football game. Take a nap. Have a family dinner. Imagine how much nicer the typical Monday would be if you really obeyed the commandment to rest and honor your Sabbath on Sunday. In fact, if we took God at his word, we would be so well rested and peaceful the next morning that Monday would not even feel like Monday anymore.

YOU ARE WHAT YOU EAT

C.S. Lewis once wrote, "...[Jesus'] command, after all, was Take, eat: not Take, understand."[5]

The Eucharist is both high majesty and true mystery. It is an inexhaustible source of grace, ripe for deep reflection and frequent reception. Why limit receiving Our Lord to Sunday Mass? Try to get to Mass during the week, maybe several times or even daily.

If your parish has an adoration chapel or Eucharistic adoration, take advantage of this opportunity to spend time in prayer before the physical presence of Jesus. There is great power in kneeling and sitting in silence before the presence of the Lord in the Eucharist, gazing upon him as he gazes upon you. Try to carve out an hour, or even thirty minutes, during the week when you can come into the Lord's presence and place all your anxieties, joys, sufferings, gratitude, and needs into his hands.

READ SCRIPTURE *FOR A CHANGE*

The word of God does not need to be intimidating. There are several accessible and high-quality resources available to

<hr>

5   C.S. Lewis, *Letters to Malcolm: Chiefly on Prayer* (New York: Mariner Books, 2002), letter 19.

help you begin reading the Bible, get more out of the Sunday readings, or just find hope for the day.[6] When we immerse ourselves in Sacred Scripture we are not only learning about God and his revelation to us, we are reminded page after page about his promises and faithfulness.

Here are some favorite verses of mine to get you started:

- Genesis 1:26-27
- Exodus 14:14
- Proverbs 3:5-6
- Proverbs 16:3
- Psalm 23:1
- Sirach 6:14
- Isaiah 41:10
- Jeremiah 29:11-12
- Matthew 6:34
- Matthew 28:20
- Mark 9:23
- Luke 9:23
- John 14:6
- Romans 12:1-2, 9-21
- 1 Thessalonians 4:3
- James 4:8-9
- 1 John 4:8
- Ephesians 2:10
- Revelation 21:4

SET YOUR WATCH TO IT

Prayer is powerful when it is spontaneous and extemporaneous. God loves quick and improvised prayers, but nothing beats having a rhythm to your prayer life. Every day can get busy and quickly get away from us. Set an alarm or a reminder on your smartphone at different times throughout the day to call you to prayer. You could set it, for example, to 9 AM to pray the St. Michael Prayer, to noon for the Angelus, to 3 PM for the Divine Mercy Chaplet or a decade of the Rosary. Then, you could end

---

6   Resources available at ascensionpress.com include *The Bible Timeline, a Great Adventure* Bible study program which presents a convenient and easy-to-follow way to read the "story" of Scripture; the books *Praying Scripture for a Change* by Tim Gray, *The Bible Compass* by Edward Sri, *Walking with God: A Journey Through the Bible* by Tim Gray and Jeff Cavins, and *A Biblical Walk Through the Mass* by Edward Sri. Also check out the various resources at biblegeek.com to help increase your comfort level and understanding of the Bible.

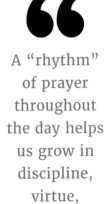

A "rhythm"
of prayer
throughout
the day helps
us grow in
discipline,
virtue,
and holiness.

the day with an Examination of Conscience at bedtime.

Of course, if you already have a robust prayer life, these suggestions may seem a little simplistic or even reductionistic. Nonetheless, the point here is that a structured rhythm of prayer throughout the day helps us grow in discipline, virtue, and holiness.

Beyond that, it is helpful to set aside a place to pray in your home. A prayer room or corner goes a long way in reminding us to pray and helping us to focus and inviting others to join us. If you are not now praying with your spouse or as a family, consider starting. Family prayer is a fruitful way to sanctify your home. Start simply, and do not worry about carving out long periods in which to pray. God cares about the depth of our prayer much more than its length.

MISSION POSSIBLE

Write a mission statement for yourself—and, if married, for your spouse and your family. Describe the person you want to become and what you would like your marriage or family to be like. Then pray often about achieving your goals. As situations arise and struggles inevitably come, go back to your mission statement to hold yourself accountable. When stresses hit, it is easy to become overly reactive to the world around us and become fearful and filled with anxiety. Having a sense of mission and purpose when days are good helps us to tread water and survive on those days we feel like we are drowning.

The more you experience God's presence in you, your home, your school, the Church, and the world, the better you will be able to share God's love with all those you encounter.

MOVING FORWARD

As we have already seen, it is vital to have a plan in place as you move forward. You have been created by God out of love, in his image and likeness. If you have been baptized, you are his son or daughter. You have been saved by Jesus' death and resurrection. You are led by the Holy Spirit, the same spirit that inspires and animates the Church.

Remember, living as a Christian is not about finding yourself. It is about finding and unleashing Christ's presence and power within you. The more you experience God's presence in you, your home, your school, the Church, and the world, the better you will be able to share God's love with all those you encounter. The secret to a joyful life and a hope filled future isn't about figuring out tomorrow, it is about listening to God today.

You are not just one of the ninety-nine; you are the "one." You are the "one" the Good Shepherd has been chasing after. You are also the "one" he wants to use to reach out to another runner, another soul desperately in need of his love and mercy.

Everyone has a story.

Our prayer is that you see the Author of Life at work in your story every day and that you enjoy every breath of this wild ride until he calls you home.

Be the one. Find another one.

Be God's.

Discussion Questions

1. In what ways are you using your God-given gifts to serve him and build up his Church?

2. Are you are doing what God designed you to do? Why or why not?

3. Is the sacrament of Reconciliation something you avoid or look forward to? What has been your experience with confession?

4. What could you do differently to reclaim your Sundays for God?

5. Are you willing to let the Holy Spirit guide your life, of handing over control to him? Why can this be difficult?

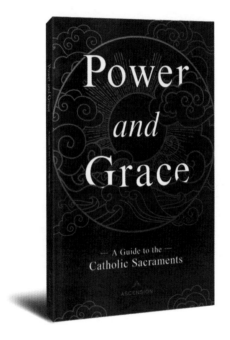